It's A Game Of Two Halves

by Frederick RJ Hartman

Foreword by Rodney Marsh

D1826098

Beaten Track
www.beatentrackpublishing.com

Beaten Track

First published 2012 by Beaten Track Publishing
Copyright © 2012 Frederick RJ Hartman

The moral right of the author has been asserted.

A CIP catalogue record for this book
is available from the British Library.

ISBN 978 1 909192 00 3

Cover Design by Beaten Track Publishing
Cover photo courtesy of Kaitlyn M. Neve Art and Photography
(www.kaitlynmneve.com)

www.beatentrackpublishing.com

For Mum (Moth). Always my number one fan. The feeling was mutual.

For Dad (Pop). It may have taken 43 years, but I wrote a book in the end, just like you always said I should.

For Queenie (HRH). Thanks for the friendship and the memories.

For Nigel (Nige). Thanks for getting me into all this thirty odd years ago. I will always have you to thank / blame.

For Kerri (The current Mrs. Hartman). Thanks for putting up with me all these years. I know I am not easy to live with (at times).

And for my Joe (Fish) and for my Katie (Mushroom). This is for you both, the two best little people that ever came into my life. I hope one day this book will help you find out what your old dad was all about and a little more about where you came from.

"Every dog has its day, and today is woof day"

– Ian Holloway

Whilst this is a work of non-fiction, there may, on occasion, be some fictional embellishment to aid the story-telling process.

Foreword

When Fred asked me to write a foreword for his new book I was only too happy to do so, because he is a lifelong QPR fan.

After reading it, it dawned on me that fans have a completely different perspective on their team than the players do. Players come and go but fans are there forever.

Simply put, Fred's book is the story of a man who grew up in a family whose life is dedicated to the R's.

It talks about his youth and his family, and his love of football and the players he grew up watching, in a humourous and, sometimes, cynical and sarcastic way. This makes it believable.

The thing that shines through during his account of the promotion season, game by game, is his passion and love for his football team.

He seems to enjoy following Rangers almost as much as I loved playing for them.

Rodney Marsh

Prologue

A love story.

No it's not like any other love: this one is different as it's not boy meets girl, or boy meets boy, or girl meets girl, or indeed any other permutation of genders walking off into the sunset happily ever after. That said, it does contain boys and girls, men and women, births, marriage and deaths. Oh, and football. In particular, one great campaign in the highs and lows of Queens Park Rangers FC, and their *NPower Championship* winning season of 2010-2011.

It's A Game of Two Halves, rather as the title may suggest, is in two halves. The First Half is a potted history of my growing up in the seventies and eighties and the effect football had throughout this time and still does to this day. The Second Half looks in detail at the 2010-2011 season through the eyes of a supporter – not one who attends every game or knows every statistic, but is no less passionate for listening to games on the radio / online stream, or catching the latest score courtesy of *Sky Sports Gillette Soccer Special* on a Saturday with Jeff Stelling – one who keeps up with news and views via websites and message boards and anxiously awaits text messages from his mate at the game while he sits at home.

This is no ordinary football yarn however, as it explores an obsession with following your team from afar (and the pitfalls of not actually being there) while looking at key relationships and interactions, and how fitting football into your everyday existence can often prove difficult. The book is about life, loves, winning and losing and the voids created by the latter when it's not just the match in question. It's about how the relationships you have stand you in good stead for life, but can also be devastating when they are no longer there.

Above all, this is a story about friendship.

Friendship. Family. And Football.

FIRST HALF

The Queen is dead, long live the Queen...

It was Saturday, June 18th, 2011. Eleven years and one whole day since my marriage to Kerri in the Millennium year. To celebrate the event (the 'one whole day' I mean: the eleven years are a celebration in themselves), I was in a greasy spoon café, a first frequent of this establishment, and a rare visit for me for a fry-up breakfast, even though my rather ample frame may suggest otherwise. We were greeted by a rather buxom and jolly lady who exchanged banter with us in a rather flirtatious way, as she seemed much used to having men go in and almost, by implication, expect more than sausage and beans to be on the menu.

Today, along with the gastronomic delights which were actually available on the rather impressive short order menu, I was catching up on events at my previous company with an old work colleague, and realised, as it is with companies and leaving them, that much is the same. Targets get tougher, people come and go, and the old adage 'same sh*t, different day' never more apt. As we tucked into numerous fried animal parts, washed down with a traditional mug of tea (milk, two sugars, mug complete with obligatory chip), I was somewhat surprised to receive a call on my mobile at this relatively early hour.

It was around 9am and it was Kerri (or who I affectionately refer to as 'the current Mrs. Hartman'). As I looked at my phone, the smiling pose of her I have whenever she calls looking back at me, my immediate thought was this is going to be the usual 'we are low on milk, can you bring six pints home when you come back', or something equally as unexciting.

"Hello, what have I got to bring home now? I'm just tucking into me rather fine pork 'n' 'erb sausages."

"Honey, you need to come home."

By the tone of her voice, it was clear this wasn't simply a request to bring home some shopping items. My first reaction was there's something wrong with the kids. She confirmed that they were OK, so I asked if it was her and again she reassured me. It wasn't that either. I agreed to go straight home. All I could think about was what the hell it might be. I made small-talk with my friend as he drove us back to mine with the slight increase in alacrity one might expect from someone who has just been told that they need to come home straight away, but who is also conscious of the national speed limit and the built up areas through which we were travelling.

On arrival, I was greeted by my daughter Katie (or Mushroom), and she said, with the simplicity and total honesty of a six year old:

"You know your friend Queenie? He died."

Paul 'Queenie' Farley, my dear friend of nearly twenty years.

Friends...

Sometimes we determine who they will be. Sometimes they kind of find us. Perhaps it's common ideals; maybe it's people you work with or neighbours. Or perhaps it's a common interest which throws you together initially, and your friendship develops from there. Well, in the case of Paul Farley and me, it was the latter, although common passion would be more fitting, for our beloved Queens Park Rangers. Back then I still had hair, a subject that would form many of the friendly 'slates' and banter that would become our trademark over the ensuing years, while Paul was always a 'big lad' (the counter 'slate' I had as my retort). Thus 'Slaphead' and 'Fatto' (a parody on Statto from Baddiel and Skinner's *Fantasy Football League* due to his immense knowledge of the game) were just two of our normal salutations.

Queenie was a larger than life character who had evidently earned this nickname during one particular verbal joust, where he had made comment of one of his peers and was told to 'Shut up Queenie!', on account of his chosen attire for the day: a t-shirt emblazoned with the group Queen. Hence, from that fateful (for him at least) day, the name stuck, making his real name of Paul Farley somewhat redundant.

Over the years I elaborated on this, thus 'Queenie' was shortened to 'Queen' and eventually 'HRH'. Indeed, as with many nicknames, they get expanded over time, my mother donning him 'The Loyal Royal', such was his fanaticism for the R's, and a reference to his not so regal connections.

Over time, Queenie and I would meet at various grounds around the country, and began to forge a friendship fuelled by our passion for all things Blue and White. I would often stay at his mum Shirley's house when I was down on business in Romford, to save the trip back to Norwich, and to allow easy access to a home match the next day. The favour would be reciprocated by my parents, when he made the annual pilgrimage for our match against my nemesis Norwich City, so my mum and dad also got to know this larger than life Hoop

9

fanatic. When I moved down to Hertfordshire for a few years, we had season tickets next to each other, in the Upper Loft, closer to the adjoining South Africa Road stand. A few seasons on and we moved to where he remained long after I was forced to stop attending, still in Loftus Road Upper, but now in Block NU, row H.

HRH in his seat

Queenie's enthusiasm continued after I was exiled back to Norwich, with regular phone contact before and after most games, where I would seek updates as to how we had played, formations, anything and everything concerned with the match. We would joke that the only thing he didn't know was the colour of the ref's underpants, although he would usually hazard a guess!

We attended some of the most important games together in the club's last ten years, from the elation of the play off semi-final second leg against Oldham at Loftus Road in 2003, followed by the disappointment of the final at the Millennium Stadium against Cardiff, to Hillsborough promotion delight in 2004. He became THE person I spoke to after every game. He was the one person who truly got what all the fuss was about. He attended the last three *Sponsors Nights* with me and my son Joe, as my 'special guest'. He still came up for the Norwich game and found a new friend in my six year old daughter Katie who seemed to treat him as a bouncy castle! And how apt that I had seen him only a few weeks ago at Birchanger Services on the M11, when he had been kind enough to collect on my behalf a signed framed shirt I had purchased from the club. He was on fine form, as usual, with plenty of the requisite banter, packed into about an hour.

It was only recently that I had received a text from a mutual friend, Jim, informing me that Paul was in hospital. Neither of us knew the severity of his illness, or that in the eight short days from him being admitted with pancreatitis, he would be so cruelly taken from us, aged just forty-four. Typical of Paul, he even sent Jim a text message asking him to sort out his season ticket, as he foresaw a lengthy stay in hospital.

I rushed into the house and there was Kerri, crying, and nodding that what I had just heard was indeed true. Now, as anyone who has ever received news such as this will know, your brain sends mixed messages around your head, ranging in kind from 'it can't be true, I was only speaking to him a few days ago' to the awful realisation that it was of course possible. I was numb. In this situation, you tend to blabber out anything – the state of the economy, the inclement weather for the time of year, the recession. So I did quite well, considering.

"What happened?" I asked, incredulous. She was standing in the kitchen, back pressed against the sink.

"His sister rang, said he had been in hospital for the past week, and that his condition just got worse, and he passed away in the early hours."

I couldn't comprehend it. Why now? Queens Park Rangers, our mutual passion, the common denominator that had made our paths cross in the first instance, had just a few short weeks previously seen their finest hour in thirty years. Promoted as Champions of the *NPower Championship* 2010-2011, for God's sake! Back in the Premier league! I poured myself a neat scotch, something that always seems justified in movies whenever there is bad news, and knocked it back in one. I knew I had to call Shirley and tell her I knew. I can't recall what I said and in fairness, whatever I was feeling she was feeling a hundred times over. I began to retell tales of our exploits to try and fill the silences. I said the things that people always say in these troubled moments, like 'if there is anything I can do, just let me know'. And I meant it, albeit that logistically, with me being in Norwich and Shirley in Chingford, East London, it wasn't going to be easy.

The rest of the day I felt physically numb. I really didn't want to speak to anyone. Well I did actually. To HRH.

To this day, I still have Queenie's phone number in my contacts, listed as 'HRH'. I don't know if I will delete it, I don't know why I don't. My rational, sensible side knows he isn't coming back, but I still leave it there, just in case. The problem is that if we allow ourselves to really get to know someone and we become close, the pain we feel when they go is, at times, unbearable. Of course, it also makes the process of remembering a lot richer, as we have our numerous anecdotes and memories to call upon, to try and make the grieving process more palatable. If we simply go through life aloof and insular, not allowing ourselves to feel anything or to have feelings about anyone, then we don't hurt. But then we don't love, and without love there is no hurt and no real reason for us to exist.

If Tarantino did films with water pistols...

I was shaken temporarily from my numbness when Katie came running in to tell me that my son Joe had fallen outside in the park and was calling for me. I made my way to where he was lying on the floor. Thankfully, he was OK. I asked what had happened and through his tears he explained that one of the other lads had pushed him off the bars and he had landed awkwardly. When I asked for the culprit, he pointed at a rather smug lad whom we had run into on a few occasions: probably no more than ten years old, but one of those lads bordering on being a bully whilst not really being cut out for the role. The verbal volley I sent his way at that moment would have made many a grown man quake! His bottom lip began to quiver as all the pent-up anger, shock, disbelief and pain erupted from within me.

I helped Joe up and we made our way inside. Had I been in possession of a magnum (the firearm, not the ice-cream bar, but loaded with double choc ice-cream) and just blown this guy away, it would have made a fitting final scene to a Tarantino movie. Just picture it, in a café rather than a play park: I would be Mr. Baldie, Joe would be Mr. Small, and this kid Mr. Smug. I walk in just as Mr. Smug is laying into Mr. Small. Only Mr. Smug don't see me enter the café, see? I amble up to him, tap him on the shoulder and he turns.

"Yea? Waddya you want, baldie?"

"That's MISTER Baldie to you, punk!" as I crack the butt of my pistol into his nose. He falls back, clutching his hooter and yelling "Mummy!!!!". I stand over him, and let him have it, water squirting out of both barrels of the *Nerf Super Soaker Scatter Blaster Thunderstorm Water Gun* I had just taken delivery of from *Amazon* that very morning, soaking the little creep to within an inch of his life.

"I hope there won't be a next time, but if there is, well... next time you might not be so lucky. Next time I won't be alone. Let's hope you never have to meet Mr. Black-Belt and Mr. Waistline. You think my Scatter Blaster is fierce? You wait and see the heavy artillery they carry. I ain't never seen no-one get up from a blast from Mr. BB's 10" willy water pistol. If the load from that don't make your eyes water then his trademark calling card of where he sticks it afterwards certainly will!!!!"

The days after the terrible news were solemn. I sought some comfort in conversations with mutual friends, as we shared many stories of the past: lads' football away trips and the lines we would have heard at one time or another. However, the ensuing days leading up to the funeral are not dissimilar to treading water. You go through the motions, dreading the day and wanting it to arrive in almost equal measure, not wanting to attend such a sad event but also knowing that it will at least give some closure to such awful proceedings.

The date was finally set for 1st July, 2011 – ironically, the last day of my planned family holiday and just a week before the Rangers players returned for pre-season training, now as a Premier League team. The funeral took place in Enfield, not far from the family home, and was well attended by friends and family, as is to be expected for such a popular and well-liked person.

My abiding memory of the day was that of the small band of friends who supported the R's, and who knew Paul, in the main, from the many away trips he had attended with them over the years. A mutual friend, James 'Jim' Luck, had arranged for a floral tribute of a wreath in the shape and colours of a QPR home shirt. Jim also gave a eulogy, along with David, Paul's solicitor and close personal friend. Both were touching and warm in their honesty. After the ceremony, many of us attended the wake, at the Royal Forest Hotel on the brilliantly apt Rangers Road, and as expected, many stories flowed. Here we were joined by 'Big' Ali – fellow Hoop and my former work colleague turned mutual friend – as we regaled tales of the infamous 'lads' away trips' over the years, with Ali often the nominated driver.

So sit back, dear reader, and take yourself a seat. This may not be uptown Jamaica, but I promise you a treat (or three) as I invite you to join me and the lads, on the road....

Our floral tribute to Paul 'Queenie' Farley

Away the lads...

One such trip saw us head 'Oop North' to Bolton and the new Reebok stadium. We were in much need of both liquid and edible refreshment, and found ourselves parked in the stadium car park, where we were told that we could go in to the adjoining pub, as long as we "didn't show colours". So, we tucked in our scarves and shirts, fastened our coats up to our collars, and made our way in. Of course we didn't stand out at all! Although there was a chill in the air, it was also mighty sunny, so the sight of six burly lads with coats done up to their chins and appearing to be mute did raise the odd suspicion among the home fraternity. And, as luck would have it, there was a nice round table we could all sit at, almost as if, for some inexplicable reason, it had been left vacant just for us, such was its location in the pub's conservatory and in direct sunlight. Within minutes of sitting down, sweat was gathering on our collective brows, and we would of course have cooled off, had we the option of taking off our coats. We did consider leaving, but with no other pubs for miles and already having paid to park, we stayed and ordered our hot meals.

After a nice wait in the sweltering sun, our food arrived, and we ate as quickly as possible, seeing as if we didn't get some air, and pretty soon, there was a chance some of us would be missing the game through heat stroke. One of our party, however, was still tucking into his fish and chips: yes, you are ahead of me, dear reader. Queenie was manfully wading through a piece of fish we christened 'Moby Dick'. He just wouldn't let the damned thing beat him, although a few chips did survive to fight another day.

The game itself was predictably uneventful and we succumbed to yet another mega annoying 1-0 defeat, the scoreline that any fan will tell you frustrates the most, as you always think you have a chance at 1-0, but you don't even get to cheer a goal, for all your valiant effort getting there, not to mention the cost or loss of body weight in the conservatory sauna.

Then there was another trip, strangely also in the north and also to a team beginning with the letter 'B' (this was to prove a theme, although on this occasion we did have something to cheer about). For me, it was like a Busman's Holiday, as Blackpool is the Great Yarmouth of the north. Queenie, Ali, Dale (an old school friend and honorary Hoop, who was really only there for the beer and the lads' day out banter) and I arrived in bright sunshine and drove along the front with the windows open playing Pigbag's *Papa's Got A Brand New Pigbag* at full pelt, the tune that has become synonymous with Rangers when they score. We didn't really get any reaction from the locals, who were too busy getting ready for a stag or hen party, I concluded later.

The match was a personal triumph for the R's Richard Langley, who scored a hat-trick in a fine 3-1 win. The song at the final whistle was "We're not going home" to the tune of *Knees up Mother Brown*, and it was true. We weren't going home, having opted to stay the night in a seedy B&B (is there any other type of B&B in Blackpool I wonder? If there are any B&B owners in or around Blackpool who run an establishment not classed as seedy, please, there is no need to get in contact, as I don't intend staying there again and besides, I quite like seedy). That evening the weather turned into force 8 gales and we were fair blown up and down the front. I think it must have been night of the hen/stag, as numerous groups braved the elements in nothing more than stockings, suspenders and high heels (and that was just the blokes), while us sad souls, still content to have come, seen and conquered were dressed in our jackets and instead sought solace in *Harry Ramsden's* renowned fish and chip restaurant.

Queenie was getting a reputation as a fish lover after our exploits in Bolton with Moby Dick, but even he declined Harry's Challenge, which it seemed, essentially, was to eat your own body weight in fish and chips in return for indigestion and a certificate that stated 'I beat Harry's Challenge'. After eating more than enough we declined the local nightlife, as it was past our 10 o'clock curfew and besides, none of us had the necessary jabs. The real fun was going to be back at base, as we now had to fit four fairly large, well fed, units into a single room. I'm not sure what was worse – sharing a bed with another bloke, or the fact that at any given moment, due to the amount of crap we had all consumed during the day in terms of alcohol and junk food, one or all of us could kill the rest of the group with a single fart. Force 8 gales may have been blowing outside, but *Hurricane Queenie* was gathering momentum indoors, and there were genuine fears that someone may get hurt! Thankfully the night passed off OK and we all lived to watch another game!

Planes, trains and automobiles...

One thing that never puts a football maniac off is adversity. In 1996, Rangers were playing in an FA Cup third round tie away at Tranmere. Queenie and I were to make the longish drive to the Wirral and met at Toddington Services as usual: the 'Gateway to the North'. However, my car encountered problems soon after and we managed to splutter into a *Mr. Clutch* in nearby Luton. The mandatory sharp intakes of breath and head-shaking ensued, whilst we could merely watch as their eyes glazed over with pound signs. It transpired that my exhaust had gone and would take at least two hours to fix.

Now, with four hours to kick-off and still over three hours and one hundred and eighty (thank you Tony Green) miles to go, we had few options. The sensible (and cheapest) one would have been to stay put, pay for the repairs and go home. But as we were both football fanatics and therefore devoid of a few brain cells anyway, the over-riding thought was we must get there, at any cost. Flying was out: Luton airport was close by, but we didn't have our passports, although on reflection when travelling North of the Watford Gap it would always be prudent to carry such a permit to cross the north/south divide. Hitching a lift crossed our minds for a few seconds, but then again, I'd seen *The Hitcher* and had a nasty notion we would end up stark naked by the side of the road, with only our Tranmere v QPR tickets to cover our modesty. The train seemed a runner, however this was long before you could punch a 'to' and 'from' into a route planner on your phone or use a Sat Nag, plus there didn't seem to be a station called Tranmere, and 'somewhere up North' didn't return any options. So we were left with the most expensive, but achievable, option: that of hiring a car for the day. We managed to get a cab (as time was against us, and neither of us were built for long walks of over five hundred yards), and found the local branch of the appositely named *Hertz*.

In retrospect, if I play devil's advocate for one moment and imagine what the guy behind the counter was seeing, I don't think I would have felt comfortable lending us a car either: two fairly big units, dressed in 'colours' and somewhat fraught and preoccupied, sweating like new recruits in a health farm.

"I need a car for today. Straight away really."

"OK Sir, we need £100 deposit and it will be £75 for the day. How many miles do you think you will be doing?"

"About four hundred."

"Going anywhere special?"

"Tranmere."

"Sorry to hear that."

"Will this take long? Only while it's not likely to be a bumper crowd where we're going, it's not like the old joke of 'what time is kick-off?' 'What time can you get here?', so they won't wait for us."

"You're QPR fans, right?"

"Yea, how could you tell?"

"Apart from the shirts and scarves, it's the harrowed and forlorn look you both have."

Eventually we were on our way and actually made kick-off, and, unlike most stories of this type, Rangers actually played as favourites and won 2-0. So, apart from the two hundred notes I had to shell out on transport, it was a good day!

The labour of love...

Over the coming years there were many memorable trips up and down the country. Anyone who follows their team, home or away, but particularly the latter, will know that it really is a labour of love. It's as much about the 'craic' as it is about the football. Male bonding, doing what men do best, whilst also proving that men can actually do THREE things at once, thus denouncing the scurrilous rumours that we can just about do ONE, when in actuality we can simultaneously watch football, drink beer and talk complete balls.

In such pursuits, taking the rise out of each other becomes an art form, relaying tales of matches past, devising 'best ever elevens' such as the *"On Me 'ead Son / Worst Hair 'Cuts' Eleven"* (see below under the cleverly entitled *"On Me 'ead Son / Worst Hair Cuts' Eleven"* section) or *"Goofiest Eleven"* (likewise, with title that doesn't give it away at all!) and the ever popular away trip classic "Who had a hit in the eighties with...????".

For some reason the latter became a firm favourite with myself and Queenie, although he always knew I was the master, with my uncanny knowledge of music from that era. Indeed, if I were to go on *Mastermind* and find myself sat in the leather chair across from John Humphrys, my specialist subject could easily be "Eighties music from 1983-1985", such is my useless talent, honed from taping the *Top 40* religiously every Sunday between 4 and 7pm on my Matsui twin tape deck. I can envisage now the host saying to me "Fred Hartman, a perfect round, 22 points, all questions answered correctly and no passes", as I make my way back to my seat smugly, my nearest challenger on a mere 13, having cobbled together a reasonable round answering questions on "Crufts winners 1990-2000".

Sadly, I do wake up from this delusion to find that coming into the final round on general knowledge, I am only 3 points behind the current leader: Michael Smedley, a retired lecturer and he of the Crufts averageness. Alas my general knowledge is woeful, and I still trail by the same 3 points as I take the walk of shame back to my chair, only to have to get out of it again and shake the sweaty mitt of the smug winner, offering congratulations through gritted teeth. I do of course exact revenge in my dream and nut Smug Smedley, leaving him holding his bloodied hooter, as I am escorted from the premises by the previously unseen security guards who have been waiting in the wings for twenty odd years, hoping something like this would happen.

The "On Me 'ead Son / Worst Hair 'Cuts' / People in Glass Houses Shouldn't Throw Stones Eleven..."

1. David Seaman (utter pony – tail)
2. Marouane Fellani (Girl's name, girl's hair)
3. Chris Waddle (missed a penalty in the World Cup, nuff said)
4. Carlos Valderrama (like being dragged through a hedge backwards)
5. Jason Lee (yes, he had a pineapple on his head)
6. Kevin Keegan (I would luv it – if you got that mop chopped)
7. Bobby Charlton (naive to think we hadn't seen the comb-over)
8. Wayne Rooney (how much for that?)
9. Djibril Cisse (all those changes have literally gone to his head)
10. Marc Bircham (actually this isn't a worse haircut – legend)
11. Mark Hateley (get that barnet sorted Mark, an embarrassment)

Goofy Teeth Eleven (well nearly)...

1. Ronaldo
2. Robert Earnshaw
3. Ronaldinho
4. Luke Chadwick
5. Peter Beardsley
6. Goofy
7. A sabre-toothed tiger
8. Esther Rantzen
9. The shopkeeper at my local *Mace* who only seems to be in on a Saturday
10. Bela Lugosi in *Dracula*
11. Jaws

Banter...

Of course the other essential of trips was the obligatory Maccy D breakfast, either at King's Cross or on the M1 at Toddington Services, and to fill the people carrier with enough tins of *on offer* supermarket lager to see the car heading for its destination on its two back wheels. On one such trip, our nominated driver was Big Ali, a man who made the none too svelte Queenie look positively featherweight by comparison. It was at this point that Queenie, sitting in the front as he wouldn't really fit anywhere else, and turning to the others behind, uttered the now immortal line:

> "Lads, I don't want to worry you, but I think the driver has swallowed the airbag!"

What a great line, and typical of the banter that ensued on such trips. I remember at that time Fred West was prevalent in all the media, and as Queenie's hair had a passing resemblance to that of said murderer, he was ascribed the moniker 'Fred West' for the duration of that trip! He would always retort by referring to me as anyone he could think of who was both famous and had a bald pate, such as former newsreader Gordon Honeycomb, or Spurs legend Ralph Coates.

"Well," I'd say to him. "I may be bald, but at least I didn't knock off my house guests."

Gordon Ramsey wouldn't be impressed...

The subject (and consumption, for that matter) of food does seem to come up a lot when travelling to football matches. The staple diet of most who travel up and down the country goes something like this.

It starts with a full English breakfast, consisting of at least two of everything on the menu, followed by lager, as early as nine o'clock. A pack-up ensures there's a ham and cheese roll or three to be devoured by mid-morning, to soak up the ale. Then there's normally a stop off at services for much needed relief and maybe a hot snack is in order, such as a beef and onion slice, to keep you going until lunchtime, by which you have hopefully arrived at your nominated destination and can therefore avail yourself of the local cuisine, usually a large doner kebab (if in town and searching out a local boozer) or a hot dog or burger if treating oneself from a near to the ground stand.

At half time, it's customary to delight in a traditional pie and a pint, hopefully locally produced, to maintain focus for the second half, although a cheeky packet of Monster Munch or a Kit Kat (four fingered is preferable as it will be at least an hour before further sustenance) can be easily hidden in the coat pocket (or maybe one in each). After the match as you filter out, you may wish to top up with a hot dog to accompany you back to the car.

Once there, further lager can be consumed back down the motorway, chomping on anything left over in your rucksack that needs to be eaten up, like quiche, scotch eggs or Starburst, before stopping en route for a (not so) bargain bucket at *KFC*. Depending on size of unit, one could conceivably look at a minimum of an eight piece, although, if hunger has set in, best make it a round dozen with a couple of sides to keep the chicken company. Now you are all set for the remainder of the journey. With any luck you will be back for last orders and can enjoy a nice chicken chow mein from your local Chinese as you stagger home. Or, for those of us that prefer more traditional after the witching hour fare, how about Queenie's favourite, the large chicken doner kebab, with no salad and just lemon juice and mayonnaise.

Tattoos...

Queenie was always very proud of the QPR tattoo he had on his leg, depicting the original badge. I occasionally reminded him that after the takeover, when our club crest was changed and thus our badge, his 'tat' effectively went out of date, therefore he needed to get a new one! He would normally retaliate with something about me getting a few 'tats' of rabbits on my head, as from a distance they would look like hares! This was typical of the banter between us. I did tell him he could seek some solace in the fact that the old badge is still the one that many Rangers fans consider to be the real deal, so it wasn't like the very funny story circulating a few years back, of a Newcastle fan who idolised Andy Cole (in more recent times having changed his name to the much classier Andrew Cole) to the extent of having a tattoo of the Geordie legend put on his leg just days before he was sold to Manchester United!

It seems that many players now have an almost mandatory tattoo sleeve on one or both arms. I'm not sure if this has actually become a requirement when a player is looking to change club. Perhaps, in addition to their footballing ability, the extent to which anyone is prepared to insert indelible ink into their skin to change the pigment in the name of art and/or individuality should be questioned. Can you imagine Sir Alex Ferguson sitting down with a probable future signing and his agent, and after agreeing personal terms saying (adopt Glaswegian accent):

"Oh, one other thing son, can you roll up your sleeves? We just need to check you have the right level of tattoos for this great club."

On showing no such body modification, the manager has to let one of the brightest talents in the game go, even though his ability was not in question; a fee had been agreed between the respective clubs, and personal terms accepted.

As the forlorn player is led away by his agent he is heard to plead in broken English:

"Pleeze. But I is having more. I is having an English rose."

"Sorry son, your footballing ability isn't in question, but

when you play for Manchester United and pull on that great red jersey, you have to have the matching tattoo sleeve(s) to go with it."

Slates, not of the roof variety...

One bout of slating which happened between Queenie and me was after a time I had needed an ECG. Queenie started proceedings with his usual panache:

"What were they looking for, to see if you HAD a heart or not?!"

I took that one on the chin and went on to explain that for the hospital to attach the various pads to my chest I needed to have it shaved, as I may be follicly challenged up top, but not so in the torso department. Queenie's follow-up was to suggest they had shaved the hair on my chest in the shape of canaries, and he would sing his own version of Baddiel and Skinner's Three Lions, substituted with 'Three canaries on his chest'. He knew how much this would wind me up, the implication that I was more a Norwich supporter than a Ranger, due to my exile to East Anglia.

My retort was to also question his loyalty to the R's, given he lived in Chingford and his local team was actually Leyton Orient, very much his second team in reality, but the one I contended he should really support. As if that didn't wind him up enough, I went on to suggest that if he was thinking of having a few more tattoos, maybe these should be on his chest and in the shape of an 'O' ('The O's' being Leyton Orient's nickname), then I would sing back to him 'Three O's on your chest'. As with most of our verbal jousts, they would end in high scoring draws (the equivalent of, say, QPR 5 Newcastle 5 in 1984).

The other notable slate was Queenie's nickname for me, that of 'four'. This was some classic cockney rhyming slang, as in full he was calling me a 'four by two', a Jew. Again, I wouldn't lose the battle by a single score, so would reply with 'five', a tenuous link to Paul Gascoigne's best mate Jimmy 'Five' Bellies, and a direct dig at Queenie's rather generous frame.

Final Score: Fred 4 Queenie 5.

The early beginnings...

Now it's fair to say that I wasn't born into a football family. My father was a sporadic follower of the great game at best, and to this day I don't actually know where his allegiances lay in the years before I came along. His only link to football was doing the pools each week. He never followed any form guide; it was simply a case of marking an 'x' against a set pattern of numbers, so effectively the early forerunner of how most people play the *National Lottery*. My mother therefore didn't have the ignominy of being a soccer widow. Indeed I myself showed no interest in football until I was about 9: my early passion was dinosaurs, and while I wasn't quite 'Harry with a bucketful', I did possess a few (not real you understand, not even I am quite that old, and besides, our garden was too small). Show me a picture of any one of them and I could tell you it's Latin or Greek name, a particularly useless skill, but one that helped me through first school. I guess in later years, my ability to spot a tune from the eighties by just listening to the first few beats was its teenage and twenty-something equivalent.

Up until then, the most I got involved with football of any kind was with a selection of 'Action Men' of varying sizes and super powers, where I imagined them as part of a special football team I had created in my own imagination. *The Six Million Dollar Man* (an early Peter Crouch who stood head and shoulders above, say, Mr. Spock) was great, as nothing could pass him in goal (the untrained eye could be forgiven for mistaking it for the metal legs of a small glass-topped coffee table), unless of course Spock was to play unfair and set his phaser to stun, as clearly he was nowhere near tall enough to perform his infamous neck pinch on such a Goliath as Colonel Steve Austin.

The other end of the pitch/rug was the away end, with the goal/sofa being guarded by *Maskatron*, who not only had the ability to shoot, but could change his face with no less than three masks, one of which was that of Colonel Steve Austin, so effectively you had the Six Million Dollar Man at both ends –

a sort of Gary meets Phil Neville (perish the thought).

Also on the team was none other than *Stretch Armstrong*, a particularly useful player, as his ability to stretch half the length of the field meant very little got past him either. One danger was that if a shot did beat him, such as a daisy cutter, it could actually go under the sofa and that could be the end of that ball, rather like when, somehow, a ball is kicked out of a stadium and some lucky chap out walking his terrier gets to take home a prized souvenir. Why anyone would want to be taking their dog for a walk when their local football ground is just around the corner and, certainly in the case of many Rangers matches, there are seats available, is beyond me, although on reflection I have sat through many matches wishing I had a pet pooch to take for a walk, rather than be sat there in the freezing cold watching Tony Scully fail to beat his man down their left side (again).

Anyway, I was lucky enough to move from the imaginary world of differing size 'Action Men' purporting to be football players, when I was bought a rather expensive set of *Subbuteo*, complete with floodlights that actually worked (not with a generator you understand, but batteries) and a main stand. Sadly I was only given enough spectators to make it look only about a tenth full, so reminiscent of an evening kick-off first round *Zenith Data Systems* cup match at Chelsea. The fact that the spectators were glued in was therefore most apt, as you surely wouldn't willingly sit through such a farce unless somehow attached to one of the old wooden seats very much against your will. The crowd was also silent, which again was in keeping with a match at Stamford Bridge and there was the occasional riot too, although in this case, it was my dog Augie clambering on the pitch, the players facing the very real threat of being trampled to death, or worse still peed on.

The pitch was like velvet and really not in keeping with the mud baths that most games were played on in those days, although an unfortunate incident with a cup of Mum's *Nescafé* left a stain which lent the pitch a pleasing muddy effect, even if the stale waft of three kinds of the finest Arabica beans for weeks after was perhaps not totally authentic of a big match. I was also lucky enough to have two teams to battle out imaginary cup finals and the like, one resplendent in red, the other blue. With me as the oversized ref, I was always confident I could get a result against myself.

For those of you not familiar with the great game of *Subbuteo*, the idea is you flick the player against the ball, thus hopefully passing it to a team mate. As time goes on, the flick becomes more of a drag and before you know it, you are actually dragging the player and the ball all the way down the pitch, bypassing innocent bystanders and smashing the ball into the net (or if you wanted the defending side to win, flinging your goalkeeper across to pull off a fantastic save). Goalkeepers were different to the other twenty outfield players in that they had a long green stick glued to their feet, unlike their team mates who kind of just stood there with their semi-oval base, looking somewhat stiff and pedestrian, simply waiting for the ball to come to them and failing to have the ability to go and get it themselves, so in keeping with many Rangers players for much of the late nineties.

Thus the goalkeepers could be the real heroes, unless of course the ball was flicked at them with such ferocity that their hands snapped off, or even worse (could there be something worse than having their hands snapped off?) they were decapitated from their base and would have to see the physio (AKA my dad, when he got in from work) to check there was no lasting ligament damage. Fortunately he was usually able to glue them back on without the need for a local anaesthetic or nine months on the side-lines (an overnight drying saw them back in the game by end of school the next day).

Back then, to plot how your *real* team was doing you would use *League Ladders*, an ingenious invention made from one big bit of card with slits, and lots of little cards that fitted into the said slits, each with the name of a league team. Each week, or after a match, you would change the order of the teams to reflect where they were in the league. This worked well until:

1. You lost a team/s card and thus the table had a blank space/s;

2. You dropped the table on the floor and most of the little cards fell out, so unless you had kept the previous weekend's paper or were *Rainman*, you had no idea where the hell to put each team's card, or, in some cases, even what league they were in.

So it was only when I started to watch The *Big Match* with Brian Moore on a Sunday afternoon with an older relative, Tibor, while visiting my cousins Ilone and Boisie (two Hungarian ladies and exceptional cooks who made Delia Smith look like a no stars chef at *McDonalds*, such was the intricacy and scope of their culinary talents) did my taste buds (football and otherwise) begin to develop.

Each Sunday, Mum, Dad and I would head over to Southgate, North London, for a gourmet feast consisting of Lord knows how many courses including dishes like luction soup, chopped liver and egg, full chicken dinner, and home-made apple strudels. After the gastronomic delights had been cleared, it was time for the afternoon siesta for some of the adults and the TV on for those who wanted it. It was then that Tibor would position himself in the best seat in the house and watch a programme which held no interest for me, but seemed to leave him transfixed. Each week I would edge nearer the telly and try to determine what all the fuss was about. I remember lying on the floor, on that old fashioned swirly patterned carpet, and watching teams like Chelsea (boo!) and Arsenal play on terribly muddy pitches, but the first team to catch my eye was the great Nottingham Forest side of the late seventies and early eighties.

Here was a team that played with passion and talent and they were relentless, particularly in Europe. I watched them win the European Cup Final in May 1979, against Malmo of Sweden, at home, on my parents' black and white television (we couldn't afford colour, although it wasn't the colour of today, more of a too yellow or too red affair I seem to recall!).

Even to this day I don't need to 'Google' that team! Peter

Shilton in goal, Larry Lloyd, John McGovern, Viv Anderson, David Needham, Gary Birtles, John Robertson, Peter Withe, Trevor Francis, Kenny Burns, Tony Woodcock, Ian Bowyer, Martin O'Neill, Frank Clark and Archie Gemmill – a player who, for some inexplicable reason, my mum cottoned onto and would always refer to as 'Ooh, me little Archie!'.

Boisie, Tibor, Ilone, Dad and Mum

Hillel House...

I started out school life at Hillel House, a Jewish private school that warranted private fees. As my folks were basically living on the breadline, they only afforded these by a combination of (I am convinced) borrowing money and helping out at the school in a cleaning capacity. The other students there were very Jewish, and stereotypically so, thus tuition fees were not a problem for those that had money. I was never a great academic: I was a 'trier', with an aptitude for English, while my creativity came from singing. Little did I realise that this talent would be utilised over years to come in football stadia up and down the country, as well as in the shower.

It was in the extremely small playground that I cut my early football playing teeth, during lunchtime matches with a tennis ball, two coats making up one goal, and painted-on white lines on the relatively high brick wall at the end of the playground making up the other. It was a game of real skill, as not only did you have to beat your opponents, you also needed to dribble round the other children playing their games on the unofficial football pitch.

From time to time, if one got a little over-excited trying to emulate Dutchman Arie Haan's (a name more in keeping with an Amsterdam lap-dancing club) wonder goal from the 1978 World Cup finals when shooting towards the wall end, the ball would clear it, and an intricate climbing manoeuvre was required, which involved:

1. Clambering onto a fence
2. Then a wall
3. Followed by the top of a phone box (bizarrely) which in turn and almost certainly
4. Wore out one or both of the knees of your trousers, before
5. Allowing yourself to drop down into an overgrown area behind the wall to retrieve the lost ball.

The way most of us began to build our knowledge of players was by collecting *Panini* stickers. At various areas around the playground, one could hear the almost mantra-like chanting of "Got. Got. Got. Need. Got. Got. Got". Early entrepreneurs came in the form of those kids who knew the worth of certain players and could get other kids to part with a 'Liam Brady' in exchange for numerous lesser mortals, thereby filling their books more quickly than the rest of us. These days you can just hop on eBay and buy the whole set before they even go on general sale! But back then the only way you could finish a book was by getting down to the last thirty stickers, and, heaven forbid, WRITE down the numbers of the stickers required, then SEND AWAY via snail mail for the remaining all-stars needed to complete the collection.

I still to this day have an *All Stars* sticker book from 1978, where I have actually put in two Arsenal players the wrong way around, so Richie Powling will always be David O'Leary, and vice versa, although I did go and cross out the names and change them in black marker pen in my bestest handwriting to make them correct, no doubt devaluing the book without changing the fact that both players will forever be stuck in the wrong places. My belated and heartfelt apologies to both. I do wonder if that was the catalyst for how their respective careers were to pan out, as I know David O'Leary went from strength to strength, but can't say I remember too much about Richie Powling.

Perhaps we all underestimated the 'Power of the Panini' in shaping the careers of many a player. I wonder how many other careers waned due to being stuck in the wrong place, or maybe in the right space but with a dog-eared corner or the sacrilege of being put in on the wonk and not within the defining parameters of the pre-marked space. Could it be that a whole team's poor performance all season and ultimate relegation was down to some small boy somewhere, not finishing his team's pages, leaving them weakened for the entire campaign on account of those remaining being stuck at odd angles, or in the wrong spaces, a la Richie Powling? Maybe that was the reason why Rangers were relegated in

1979. Or maybe it was just because they were not good enough.

While I was merely an average player who really just enjoyed the game, I was world champion at hand tennis, a self-proclaimed title obtained by beating my friend Victor, a French Canadian, hence an overseas player, making the victory worthy of international accreditation. The artful game of hand tennis consisted of hitting the ball against the wall with your hand, often the same wall that doubled as a football goal, so at times the tennis world championship could be going on at the same time as the world cup final, on the same pitch, with two tennis balls, with the added possibility of 'kiss chase' interrupting proceedings. I'm not sure that during a proper football match you would have been able to simply walk out of the game to take up your position in a world hand tennis match and for this in turn to be interrupted by the prospect of being snogged by Michelle Grayson (my first crush at around the age of eight).

I don't remember too many incidents of a sort of institutionalised racism, but I do remember one lad calling my mother something, and having to ask my dad what it meant. When I mentioned the word 'Shiksa' he got slightly irate (quite rare for my dad as he was actually quite a calm character, having I think been a bit of an 'angry young man' in years gone by) and once he had explained it, even I, a very placid kid, was none too happy. I remember being at school again and the same lad making a point, during some argument, that I wasn't really Jewish as my mum was a 'Shiksa' and this being like a red rag to a bull. A brief playground scuffle ensued, and as the boy went down on his knees, I swung a kick at him, which caught him in the mouth, chipping his tooth. I was sent to the headmaster's office, while the lad was being cared for and having his mum called. My parents were called too. This was most out of character for me and when they arrived they were told what had happened, but instead of being in any kind of trouble, once the background as to why the fight had occurred was clarified, I was merely told off by the Head and that was the end of it.

The truth of the matter was that 'Shiksa' referred to a non-Jewish woman and by implication, meant that my dad had married out of his parent's faith and broken tradition; thus I wasn't Jewish and shouldn't be allowed in the school. My parents were actually proud that I stood up for my mum; indeed, she had offered to change her faith over to that of Judaism when they married, but it was my father who had been against it, citing that he married my mother for who she was, not her religion. However, it had been a dying wish of my grandfather that I follow the Jewish path, hence my attendance at a Jewish Primary school, and my study at a local synagogue in Wembley from the age of around eleven, in preparation for my Bar Mitzvah at the age of thirteen.

This ceremony would normally act as the confirmation of taking the Jewish faith, but in my case it was only the first part of the process, as Mum's lack of the religion meant that I would have to have a further ceremony at the age of fourteen, to effectively be confirmed as Jewish. This however never came to pass, as we moved to Norwich and I never took the final part of the process. Not that I have any regrets about my almost floating beliefs, I really feel that you must follow your heart on this one, and if religion offers you spiritual enlightenment, then it's fine to believe in what you want to believe in. Where I do have an objection is when people's religious views are effectively shoved down your throat. It's little wonder that when much of what happens around the world is driven by such extreme views, I don't feel I have missed out too much by not having a faith as such.

I say a little prayer for you...

I guess I can't really be too surprised that when I do say a little prayer to any mighty force on high for a Rangers result that it goes unheeded! There, I guess, is the irony of religion. We can't expect divine intervention to be turned on like a tap at our convenience, and besides, why should me praying for three points on a cold February afternoon at Craven Cottage be more important than some sad Fulham soul praying for a home win in the same game? I sometimes think that God has to look at all the home supporters all over the world, weigh up the sort of week each and every one has had (did they do the right thing by themselves, their families, their friends and of course God himself?) and compare this against all the supporters of the away team (not that I'm saying he collates all this data himself, I'm sure he has others to help. And an *Apple Mac*).

He probably has some advanced points scoring system, such as 'helped an old lady across the road = one point' or 'raised his middle finger to a fellow driver who didn't say thank you for waiting = minus one point'. That said, if the old lady didn't actually want to be escorted across the road, and you were merely dragging her in the hope that this gesture would con the 'officials' into thinking you were carrying out an act of kindness and not in fact to score an all important point, then of course a point could be deducted for what, on the face of it, seemed like a noble act, with maybe a further one taken away for veering the poor old dear off her chosen route AND not even having the common decency to put her back to square one.

The cleverer among you may realise that this is actually a double points opportunity, thus: taking an old lady (or man, it has to be said, for discrimination of this form would surely call for a points deduction in itself) from one side of the road to the other and then back again secures two points, but only if the said old personage actually wanted assisting anywhere in the first place. Likewise, the driver who didn't acknowledge that a car had waited for him would also see a one point deduction, and of course if he counteracted the middle finger gesture of

39

the other motorist with a similar one fingered retort, then he could also see a further point deducted. Add to that a potty-mouthed expletive and the good Lord could take off three points, plus a further two for making the hat-trick.

The more convinced I become that God has some sort of system like this, the more I think that I may have singlehandedly forced Rangers to defeat in many games in the nineties due to my, at times, uncontrollable road rage. I'm sure there were days when my points tally for middle fingers, swearing like a trooper and general unpleasantness to fellow road users completely negated all the positive scores that those assisting grannies across busy highways had achieved. I guess once all the scores are in, God can then determine which teams are going to win that day, and even have a cheeky flutter knowing the outcome. Of course, as it's His game, He could do this, but clearly if it were one of his loyal subjects back down on planet earth seen in 'Bet Fred', parting with a few quid on a pre-determined result, this act of cheating would surely be a points dockable offence. It does make you wonder if the good Lord actually has a soft spot for any team in particular, though I guess on balance if this is the case, He is probably sitting on a cloud in a red shirt with *Aon* emblazoned on it. I bet He never has to wait for His replica shirt to come into the club shop AND I'll wager His size is always readily available.

Of course, the main problem with such a system is that if your team is followed by a group of degenerates, then they are dragging down the score each week, before the do-gooders can even get going. Plus, if that were true, why have Chelsea done so well in recent seasons? And that's not the only flaw. I mean, if we played Manchester United, who have millions of fans worldwide, is it fair that they have so many more opportunities to pick up points for remembering their wives'/girlfriends' birthdays and thus claim thousands of extra points just by weight of numbers? OK, the remembering wives/girlfriends analogy is a poor one, as I'm sure the numbers here are very low, and if what they bought was the wrong size, or bought for their own benefit anyhow (like sexy undies) or just plain unromantic, like a *Dyson*, then points would be deducted anyway.

I dread to think what unspeakable acts of terribleness Rangers fans must have been up to on Tuesday 26th November, 2002, when we lost to Vauxhall Motors in the FA Cup. Then again, perhaps God has a different system altogether for the FA Cup, given we've lost nearly every game we've played in the last ten years. Regardless, I for one am always on the lookout for grannies on busy streets these days, in the hope I can amass some points and do my bit to help Rangers to that all important result on Saturday afternoon (or Sunday lunchtime/teatime, Monday, Tuesday or Wednesday night, if *Sky* have got their way).

How I started watching the R's (or 'The Sliding Doors' effect)...

It was an event in 1979, just 32 days before the European Cup Final, that was to start my still on-going love affair with another club: one not as fashionable as the illustrious stars from Nottingham, well certainly not since the Halcyon days of a few short years before, when they challenged the mighty Reds of Liverpool for the old First Division title and fell just short in 1976. This team was battling relegation and one I knew nothing about, as I, like so many others back then (as is still prevalent in the youth of today), backed The Winners: the club with the best players, the one likely to be up there challenging for trophies. So when my best friend Nigel, some 3 years older than me, asked if I wanted to go with him and his granddad and see our local team play, I checked with my mum, and permission granted, we set off on the short journey across West London, in Nigel's granddad's black taxi cab, to see Queens Park Rangers FC.

Memories of the game are scarce for me, although I do remember a certain Mr. Clive Allen scoring a hat-trick, and me jumping up and out of my seat in the Paddocks on five separate occasions, as the Hoops ran out 5-1 winners! And although history will show that the R's did indeed succumb to the bitter reality of relegation that season, my lifelong addiction to this little West London club had well and truly begun.

Up until this game, my experience of watching football was confined to Sunday afternoons at Ilone's or for the FA Cup Final, which I used to watch at Nigel's as he had a colour television – that and the fact I enjoyed his company and looked up to him as you may a big older brother. Cup Finals were really special back then, with coverage starting mid-morning and running right up until kick-off. I loved to watch the build-up, the coaches leaving the hotel, and to think this was all just two miles away from where we were! If you came out of Nigel's house on Denzil Road, turned right onto Neasden Lane, carried on up the hill towards Neasden tube station and looked out over the railway sidings (the sidings that the *Daily Mirror* once reported were the proposed site for a future *Olympic Games* no less, and to this day are still, well, rail sidings) on a clear day you could see the famous Twin Towers in the distance. Indeed, when a goal was scored, the roar from the 98,000 capacity crowd would easily carry those two miles.

Somehow that stadium, sat imperious in the distance, was something you aspired to. Neasden itself wasn't exactly Mayfair, while Wembley had a certain opulence, so a move, even those two short miles, would see you jump from relative lower working class poverty to middle class affluence in one short tube stop on the Jubilee Line. Wembley had seen it all. 1966 no less. It was an iconic landmark and one I hoped one day to visit with the R's. The closest I had got to it was occasionally on a Sunday, where I would visit Wembley Market, the stadium standing tall only a few feet away. It was here that I purchased my first vinyl on which to cut my eclectic teeth, so to speak: the rather diverse sounds of Madness with *One Step Beyond* and Queen's *Jazz*. Sadly I was just too young and too late to feel the full force of Two Tone (although I was to revisit it some years later), but lucky enough to hit the eighties with sufficient maturity to become somewhat of an after-dinner bore on music from that era.

I would often stay over at Nigel's house on a Friday night, to help with his paper round on a Saturday morning. He

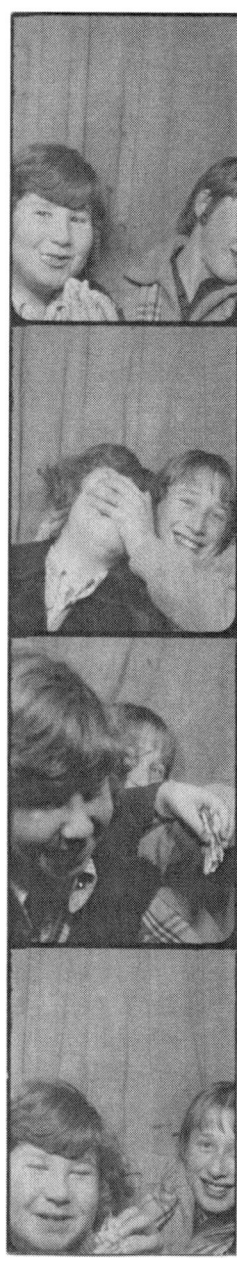

Me and Nige

43

was also well into his music, and I vaguely remember his room, mirrored like some seventies discothèque, his record decks and his vinyl collection.

We even played in some football tournament or other over at Brent Leisure Centre during one school holiday, the sort of makeshift team that is made up of kids shipped off for the day, complete with packed lunch consisting of a sandwich made with *Shiphams* beef and ham paste, a tangerine, a carton of apple juice and a *Penguin* bar (the latter invariably having melted by the time you came to eat it). It was a day out for the kids (and a day of peace for the parents) who just enjoy football for the fun of it and haven't entered the tournament to actually win it, so devoid of any skill whatsoever, other than Nigel passing a ball to me and me shouting "DUUUUCCCKKK!!!!" and leathering the sweetest right foot strike I have ever hit (to this day, in fact) into the top left hand corner. (Have you ever noticed that some people call that the top right hand corner, as in that would be the top right hand corner for the goalkeeper as he looks out? Moot point, but I just wanted to make it clear for all of you out there trying to visualise my greatest ever goal that it definitely went into the top left hand corner as I look at it!) It was a great moment in an otherwise drab match that we lost by something resembling a cricket score, against five other boys who clearly believed they would go on to bigger and better things than winning a rather poor five-a-side tournament against Makeshift Misfits United.

I further honed my limited footballing skills by playing in the street out the front of our one-bedroom maisonette in Neasden. Not only did you get to pit your wits against the kids in our street (boys and girls), but you learned to dribble in and out of parked cars, with the added bonus of dodging the moving ones that would appear round the corner every so often. I remember on one occasion when I was in goal, I threw the tennis ball we were playing with in the air and to a friend. He nodded it backwards and his mate hit the sweetest volley ever (not as sweet as my strike into the top left hand corner of the goal discussed in the previous paragraph but sweet nonetheless) – only I somehow dived to my left to turn it round the lamppost that made a rather handy (if not hugely oversized) goalpost (the crumpled tracksuit top that made up its counterpart was somewhat smaller in stature). It was my finest and only notable moment as a goalkeeper, maybe not Gordon Banks saving from Pelé in the 1970 World Cup (before my time of course) but easily the best save that Southview Avenue had ever seen and every bit as satisfying I don't doubt.

I just wonder, if Nigel and his family had been Spurs or Arsenal, or, God help us, Chelsea fans, and had taken me along that day to see them, would the love affair have been any different? Would the passion, the elation of those special days to come, or the bitterness of relegation and administration, been any better or worse? It's something I will never know for sure, but would I want to change anything, looking back at the success these clubs have enjoyed over the past 30 years, in comparison to the sparse times my own club have faced? Not a bit of it!

Even five years on, exiled from my beloved Hoops, when I went to Carrow Road to watch Norwich City, it wasn't to support them; it merely served to fill the Saturday void, to engage with the physical act of the beautiful game, albeit at a time when their team was managed by Ken Brown and blessed with great talent. This was at a time when they were still in the First Division (now the Premiership), playing against the big clubs – Liverpool, Manchester United and Arsenal and so on – with mixed success. Steve Bruce and Dave Watson were at the centre of defence, with the mercurial brilliance of Mick Channon up front, while pace was provided on the wings through Mark Barham and Louie Donowa. Add in the midfield steel of Peter Mendham and they weren't a half bad side.

Cut me in half (don't – it's a figure of speech and besides, I wouldn't live to tell the rest of the tale) and I bleed red (obviously) and blue and white (perhaps not so obviously). As any fan will tell you, once an allegiance to a team is in place, be it the family line, or, indeed how I had chanced upon it, through friendship, then you never veer off the chosen path.

You make your own luck...

I may have watched the European Cup Final a month or so later, but I was now 'switching' allegiance from the red of Forest to the blue and white hoops of QPR, and looking forward to seeing how my new heroes would perform in the old Second Division after their demise from the top flight. Again, I don't really remember much in the way of statistics (this will please many for whom the thought of yet another book on football, scores, scorers and statistics will bore the proverbials off them), but I do remember standing on the terraces at the 'School End' and being pushed in a mad surge forwards every time Rangers scored.

As time went on, Nigel and I would go further back so as not to get crushed at the front, although not being that tall meant that many matches were seen between other people's heads. While the enjoyment of the game wasn't great, the atmosphere generated when standing, swaying and chanting with the crowd is somehow intoxicating, and, as many have said over the years, there is no substitute for actually being there.

My only real (yet still somewhat vague) memory of that season was QPR trouncing Burnley 7-0, but with the passage of thirty-odd years since that game, I don't actually remember if I was there on the day or not! Rangers seemed to win their fair share of games, but if we did happen to be down and in need of some form of divine intervention, I always had my trusty red and white silk Rangers away scarf. The trick here was to take it out towards the end of a game, and if Rangers were in need of that extra help, hold each end ever so tightly and pray. I found by closing my eyes for about thirty seconds, then opening them again (I didn't want to miss the obvious goal that this new-found ritual was bound to provide) I would initially see stars. Once they'd cleared, the net would bulge as Clive Allen, or Mike Flanagan maybe, would score and send us home happy that we had at least salvaged a draw. At some point there must have been a game where my following 'the ritual of the lucky scarf' failed to produce the all-important goal, perhaps providing my first insight into there not actually being such a thing as a lucky scarf, or lucky heather, or lucky rabbits' feet (not particularly lucky for the poor rabbit, although he/she would at least have rights to park closer to the ground if displaying the correct disabled badge).

My fondest memories were actually after the games, when Nigel and I would make our way down the Uxbridge Road to catch our bus home, but before the short journey we would stop off at the *KFC* and devour our tea, one piece of the Colonel's special recipe chicken and the long since extinct barbeque spare rib, to this day the greatest rib I have ever tasted! I guess that special secret recipe somehow got destroyed in a fire and was never seen again. Many have tried since. All have failed to live up to that incredible tangy taste.

Read all about it...

The journey back home on the bus also allowed us the chance to read the all-important match day programme, which after a few hours of holding, sweating, cheering, folding and jostling was only just keeping its shape. Over the years I have collected many programmes, most from matches I have personally attended, but some bought from collectors, purchased online or even from huge factories where I can imagine being unable to walk around in there, such are the copious, ceiling-high piles of programmes. However, a genuine programme should really include all of the following:

1. Fingerprints embedded into the front and back cover from clutching it so tightly at moments of excitement/anxiety that it has taken your fingerprint, and, should you ever be accused of the murder of a fellow fan during or after the game, would leave you bang to rights. No doubt about it, the weapon of a rolled up QPR v Wrexham match day programme is yours.

2. A crease down the middle (at the very least), where it has been folded in half and shoved in your back trouser/inside jacket pocket.

3. The half/full time scores and scorers (fairly) neatly marked on the relevant page (usually the back) in blue biro, as well as team changes and substitutes.

4. May also have teeth marks from where you have EITHER clutched the programme while you were holding a coke in one hand and a hot dog in the other, then realised that you had no hands left to fold it up and put it in the aforementioned trouser/coat pocket in order to eat your hot dog or drink your coke and you couldn't even ask someone to help as your mouth was stuffed full of finest Saturday afternoon reading material; OR midway through the second half the combination of hunger and anxiety caused you to chew on a corner, having long since run out of fingernails, and the prospect of chewing off your hand

down as far as the elbow just didn't appeal, as you figured you may need it in future weeks, not least to hold a *KFC* barbecue spare rib on the journey home.

All change...

A significant thing that happened to me – one which was to cause a change in my footballing routine – was when I stopped going to games with Nigel. It happened after we had been split up during a match, with Nigel staying towards the back of the terraces, and me going to the front, to gain a better vantage point. After the game was over, Nigel was nowhere to be seen, so I was left to get home by myself, by bus, the five or so miles. After finally arriving home safely, my mum never allowed me to go to games with Nigel again, and indeed, our friendship ended for nearly thirty years. This parting of the ways should never be underestimated.

Nigel was the older brother I never had; indeed I was an only child, first born and only son of David 'Derrick' and Beryl Agnes Hartman. There were seventeen years between my folks: Dad always maintained he lived a bachelor lifestyle, drinking, gambling and playing snooker to all hours, while working for his father in his pleating business; Mum had muddled through life, working in shops; both were ready to settle down at their respective times of life. Dad was fifty-two when they married, stating his only ambition left was to sire a son, while Mum was thirty-five, and back in the Sixties having children at this age and beyond was very much frowned upon. They had known each other through mutual friends for some years, and I absolutely believe that they were perfectly suited to each other. They married and I was born shortly after (hell, there was no time to hang around, let's face it!), and both had what they had always truly wanted.

Me and Mum   *Me and Dad*

51

Me and my dad...

With Nigel now no longer a friend, I was at a temporary loss, not able to go to games, until, that is, my dad decided that he would attend matches with me. This would have been around 1981 and with the development of the ground, there was now seating upstairs in the School End, above where I had stood previously, giving a great vantage point so that the whole pitch could be seen in its entirety. Dad and I would sit up there in all weathers, he wrapped up in a scarf and big leather coat, the half time treat hot soup served from a thermos flask, and buttered rolls that Mum had lovingly prepared for us. I would always go mad when Rangers scored, whereas Dad was a lot more reserved, but he knew what it meant to me and was just happy that I was happy. I always loved John 'Budgie' Burridge, our larger than life goalie, and Bob Hazell, our huge centre back, or the 'Rock of Gibraltar' as my mum had donned him. Dad always liked Gary Waddock for his tenacity in the middle of the park.

After the games, we would make our way along South Africa Road to a small parade of shops that included a bookies and a newsagent. In the far left corner was the imaginatively named 'South Africa Road Fish Bar'. (Lord knows how long it took someone to think that one up. I can imagine these rather portly fellows sitting round one evening, having decided that what the estate needed was a fish and chip shop, to help the residents with their dietary requirements, seeing as the blowing of the remainder of their hard earned giro on who was going to win between Chelsea and Rangers and intoxication by cheap liquor and fags was already covered by next door.)

We would often have to queue out the door, and once inside, you had work your way around the counter, first to the right, then along, before finally getting your chance to speak your order to the portly Greek proprietor. It was the perfect treat to end what had hopefully been a win for the R's. With fish and chips three times (me and Mum with the cod variety and Dad with a plaice on the bone, which always took longer to cook and had to be specially prepared) secured and nestling nicely in Dad's holdall, we would continue down to White City tube station, then take the fifteen or so stops back to Neasden, via Baker Street, for our supper.

I guess looking back on it, this was the classic 'father and son' bonding, although at the time I never fully realised it, and it is only when you have kids of your own you can appreciate how it was for your father back then. Even though I was at an age where I could have idolised footballers, looked up to them as role models, or even icons, the only man I have ever truly fully respected and wanted to be like was my own dad. Unlike most footballers, he never saw the need to spit for the sake of it. He was funny, quick-witted, intelligent (not in an academic sense, but worldly-wise), loyal and completely dependable. He was always there for me, along with my mum: my greatest supporters.

Meanwhile, on the pitch, there was no doubt the team was improving, and when season 1981-82 came around, it culminated in our first and only (to this day) FA Cup Final appearance at Wembley, an all-London affair against the mighty Tottenham Hotspur.

William Gladstone...

My secondary school was a shortish walk away from my house, achieved by walking to the end of my street (away from the rail sidings and Neasden station), crossing over Dudden Hill, and cutting across Gladstone Park, home many Saturdays to our footie matches.

Me at Gladstone Park

At school, I was part of a little known lunchtime team of three, the other two players being Heidar and Rohit, both Liverpool supporters (yes, shock horror, two lads living in London and supporting the team that is doing well year after year. Go forward fifteen years and replace 'Liverpool' with

'Manchester United'). Even though outnumbered by reds two to one, I still managed to get the lion's share of the name we gave ourselves, thus Liver Park Rangers were formed. We took on all-comers at playtimes, honing our fine skills with the tennis ball with which I had learned my trade back at Hillel House. When challengers came in the form of teams of more than three, we would draft in extra recruits, but regardless of whether these guys were supporting of either the reds or the blue and white hoops, they found themselves unable to hijack the name of our team. We were founder members after all, so there was no chance of us ever becoming LiverArse Rangers or LiverSea Park

Games were frenetic, with me usually providing a running commentary throughout the game, something I had picked up from the great Brian Moore and my Sunday watching of *The Big Match*. During one particularly tense world cup final between Liver Park Rangers and a Rest of the World five, I found myself playing the back four and goalkeeper, while Rohit covered centre midfield, with Heidar the lone striker. I believe we had drafted in the guile and craft of Jitesh on the wing (by 'drafted' I mean we were short two men and he did say we could use his football, kindly brought in from home and much more fitting for a world cup final after all) along with some lad called Martin, a sporadic player with no neck – a predecessor to QPR's Andy Impey many years later.

While watching the battle in front of me unfold, I was approached by a girl from my class (whose name escapes me, but for the purpose of this I shall call Maxine, for no other reason than that it's quite a nice name and girls were called Maxine back then. I think). Maxine asked me if I supported QPR, which I confirmed to be the case and awaited the customary response of 'QPR? More like Quarter Pound of Rubbish', accompanied by sniggers from all those within earshot. Instead she told me she supported Chelsea. I should clarify that Maxine was quite tall for her age and dressed a bit like a skinhead, only without the skinhead, so I naturally put two and two together at this point and assumed I was about to get decked – a thought made all the more horrific by the fact:

1. She was a girl

2. And a Chelsea supporter

3. Given the above, I felt that a comment not dissimilar to 'QPR? Quarter Pound of Rubbish...' was even more likely to emanate from her lips

4. I was supposed to be concentrating my efforts on being the back four AND rush goalkeeper in a tense World Cup Final.

As it transpired, she reached inside her pocket and pulled out a badge with the words 'I Support QPR' on it. She handed me the badge and smiled.

Hindsight is a wonderful thing, so looking back I now realise this was a girl actually showing an interest in me. Not since Michelle Grayson had snogged me when I was eight had a girl even come near me, and nor would they again for about another six years. Indeed, a friend once said that if I was sitting in a room alone, with only one way in and out, and in walked a girl, completely naked, her eyes transfixed on me as she walked over to where I was perched, sat astride my lap and said 'Take me, take me, big boy', I would be turning round to see who she was talking to, so lame was I at spotting even the most obvious of signals from the opposite sex.

"Thanks," was all I managed to say, turning as red as a fire engine's bodywork, just as a thirty-five yard rocket whistled past me into the imaginary net and put us a goal down with just seconds of normal time (well lunchtime anyway) remaining. It was so annoying conceding a goal like that, even more so that it was hit with such power that it meant I had to run bloomin' miles to retrieve the ball. By the time I got back to goal, Maxine was gone, never to be seen again (well, not until next lesson). In the distance the whistle blew for full time and Liver Park Rangers had lost the all-important World Cup Final to an all-star Rest of the World five, but at least we didn't have to wait another four years to compete, not with afternoon break just a couple of hours away anyhow.

Bitter sweet FA (Cup) 1982...

Rangers had reached the final the hard way, or in other words, playing crap and having to get through with the assistance of replays. We started out against Middlesbrough at Loftus Road, a game that I attended, but were only able to draw 1-1, so it was back to Ayresome Park for a replay which I was convinced we would lose, but we somehow won (after extra time, if memory serves me correctly), with the result coming through on the TV at home, on the 'News at 10'. When I heard this I literally leapt down the passage of our tiny one-bedroom maisonette, shouting and screaming, pausing only to perform forward rolls, which I was quite good at, although I appreciate cart wheels would have been more impressive, but something the lack of both ability and space prevented me from doing.

The house itself was very small (but didn't have woodchip on the wall, before you start humming the next line in your head): Mum and Dad let me have the only bedroom, while they, each night, would open up a sofa bed in the front room to sleep on. My bedroom was off to the left of the hallway and the living room/Mum and Dad's makeshift bedroom was second left. I didn't like the dark much, so at bedtime would insist upon my parents leaving the living room door slightly ajar, just so it let a little light into my room from the hall. It didn't help that I had a fascination with horror movies, and scared myself half to death one night when watching *Halloween*, alone in my bedroom, on a 14 inch portable black and white TV; the fact that the indoor aerial made the picture and the sound distort seemed only to add the atmosphere of the movie.

In front was the bathroom, rarely used for bathing as it, like the rest of the house, wasn't heated, so baths for me were generally taken in the living room in an old fashioned tin affair, with a small heater to save you from hypothermia. Off the living room was the kitchen, and that was it, apart from a small courtyard garden with a whopping great set of iron steps leading to the maisonette upstairs.

The lack of garden and intervention of metal steps made backyard football very difficult, not to mention that there was hardly room to swing the proverbial cat, or in our case our beloved pet dog Augustus (or Augie as we knew him). We had Augie for about eight years from a pup, a cross breed, although I really can't remember what breed crossed with what, a bit like me and cars now. A friend will ask 'What sort of car do you have?'. 'A blue one' is the kind of retort I may give, not because I am trying to be clever. I haven't a clue, something I put down to missing school the day we discussed 'Makes and models of cars so when you are all grown up you can stand in a pub and talk about such things for hours with your mates'. Fortunately I made it in on the day we discussed 'Football and the pivotal part it will play in your life, leisure and loves, so when you are all grown up you can stand in a pub and talk about such things for hours with your mates'.

Sadly we lost Augie. Not as in he died, we literally lost him, as he escaped under the back gate during a particularly violent thunderstorm, never to be seen again, a la Richey from the *Manic Street Preachers*, only without the Vauxhall Cavalier and Severn Bridge. Maybe he hopped on the nearby Neasden tube and took the Jubilee Line to Wembley, in preparation for Rangers returning there one day.

Augie

Round 4 saw us draw 0-0 away at Blackpool but win the replay convincingly 5-1, which I can't remember attending. In the fifth round we defeated Grimsby 3-1 at Loftus Road (which I did attend). Round six and we edged a 1-0 nervy affair against South London rivals Crystal Palace. I remember going bonkers when we scored and hugging some random stranger next to me, much to my dad's chagrin. He told me to calm down! How could I? We were in the FA Cup semi-final!

The match was played at Arsenal's iconic Highbury stadium, our opponents West Brom much fancied to win, with their star striker Cyrille Regis gunning for us. The turnout that day was amazing. I had never sat in such a big stadium with so many people, a huge, noisy and colourful turnout from West London cheering the lads on. My dad and I were joined by my school friend, Heidar, who still purported to support Liverpool, but was definitely a Hoop for the day. It was an incredibly tense match. Clive Allen scored for Rangers in the second half when the ball ricocheted off his knee and into the back of the Albion net and Highbury erupted, as did I, briefly, before collapsing in my wooden chair and promptly bursting into tears! But Rangers hung on and soon we were Wembley bound! That night, as Dad and I returned home, I sang all the way down our street "Que sera, sera, whatever will be, will be, we're going to Wembley, que sera, sera". On hearing this, my mum opened the front door, and I continued to serenade her with my dulcet tones!

For the Final itself, I went to Heidar's to watch the match, again the allure of colour over black and white too strong. I was under strict instructions from Heidar (on behalf of his parents) not to jump around or go mad if Rangers did happen to score, so I sat quietly in their very well presented living room as the game unfolded. Rangers were resplendent that day in a red kit, along with a blue and white hooped tracksuit top for this very special occasion. Spurs were the better side, as expected, and a tense game went into extra time, largely thanks to a fantastic and heroic 'man of the match' goalkeeping performance from Peter Hucker.

With just ten minutes remaining, Spurs scored through Glen Hoddle and that seemed to be that. Five minutes to go and Rangers had a throw, taken by Simon Stainrod. His effort was met by big Bob Hazell, who flicked the ball on and there was Terry Fenwick, steaming in from the back to put Rangers level. 1-1! It was Heidar who went mad first, totally forgetting his own parents' advice, but swiftly followed by me, unable to contain my absolute delight! We bounced around the living room as if we had actually won the cup!

The game ended and a replay was required. I again watched at Heidar's, and it was Spurs who took the lead, an early penalty converted, again by Hoddle. Try as we might, we couldn't gain parity, and so our only ever FA Cup Final appearance was to end in disappointment. I shed a tear that night. We had thrown everything at Spurs but it just wasn't to be in the end. Little did I realise that in four years we'd be making a return to Wembley, in the Milk Cup Final of 1986, odds-on favourites to beat Oxford United.

Up sticks to the country...

My parents had made a decision: in order to clear their outstanding mortgage and have some semblance of a quiet life, we were relocating to what had been our holiday destination for the last ten years. Every summer, in August, we would head to the Norfolk coast to the same *Green Farm* resort in Scratby, for three weeks in a caravan. Geoff, the site owner, would welcome us like long lost relatives, and indeed would aim to provide the same caravan year on year: the one slotted into a corner of the site, near to the toilet block. It was literally like owning our own caravan with en suite toilet facilities long before caravans had toilets full stop, let alone those of an en suite persuasion.

With Dad almost retired and increasingly weary of the rat race that was The Capital, I was to leave behind my friends and my football team and so, when I was fourteen we moved to Norwich.

The next few years proved difficult in terms of me being able to actually see the team, but I did support them from afar, listening in at every possible opportunity on the *BBC World Service*, grabbing any snippet of info I could lay my ears on. Indeed our proudest moment since our historic League Cup Final victory against West Bromwich Albion at Wembley in 1967, where we, as a lowly Third Division club and finding ourselves 2-0 down, defied all the odds and came back to win 3-2, was the very next season, when we won the old Second Division title in 1982-1983. I remember hearing the *BBC* deliver the news via my old radio while I was sitting in the bath, in the unheated bathroom of our terraced house on Silver Road, in the north of Norwich City. However, my cravings for live football had to be nourished somehow, so for the next few years I got my footie fix by making the epic journey 2 miles south to Carrow Road to watch Norwich City. My dad was working there as a steward, in return for which he was paid the princely sum of £10 or could choose to receive two £5 seat tickets. He invariably took the latter, thereby allowing myself and my school friend Dale to attend, or sometimes my mum would come along, as she too enjoyed the odd game. At half time I would always listen out intently for the Rangers scoreline, and then again at the end of the match, as we made our way around the perimeter of the pitch to exit. The most amazing of these occasions was when we played Newcastle in 1984, and at half time we trailed 0-4! I remember Dale consoling me at the time and saying "It's OK, you will come back in the second half!" Friend he may have been; fool he most certainly was, or so I thought! At full time and as we traipsed out of the ground, the score came over the tannoy – 3-4 – but the game was still playing! I certainly perked up at this point, then within a minute the announcer declared "And it's now all over at Loftus Road, where it's finished QPR FIVE Newcastle FIVE!"

The next few seasons saw my continued fascination with the Hoops from afar, where a combination of age, lack of finance and distance didn't permit me to attend any games for MY team, although I still continued to watch the Canaries at Carrow Road. Rangers' next match of note was the aforementioned Milk Cup Final in 1986 against Oxford United. In a game touted as a nailed-on victory for Rangers, the form book was turned upside down and I again had to endure the agony of watching us lose a major final, this time by a 3-0 scoreline. I watched the game in my living room with my folks and was disgusted with our inept performance that day. I also appreciated that getting to a final was a major achievement for a club of our stature, and that it may be some time before we made it there again (and how true that prophecy was to prove).

Many people have asked me (for 'many', read at least one) why, having watched Norwich City for a few years have I come to loathe them over time? While a very simple question, it is somewhat more of a complex answer. Firstly, I don't loathe them: strongly dislike is how the thesaurus offers an alternative. I think the reason lies more with the fact that many of their fans seem to think they are better supported and a bigger club somehow than Rangers. It always seems to escape them that the only team within fifty miles of Carrow Road is

Ipswich, and that's in a different county. Quite simply, if you want to watch top flight football, Norwich have kind of cornered the market in East Anglia. I also think that, in some crazy, mixed up way, it was Norwich that kept me from my beloved Rangers for those formative teenage years, so invariably they have become my irrational team of hate. On a more basic level, any team that plays in yellow and green and has a small songbird in the finch family originating from the Macaronesian Islands as a mascot are always going to niggle even the most tolerant of football following feathered creature lovers.

Circumstances changed somewhat for me at the end of my teens, as work shipped me off to Stevenage, so I was now logistically within reach of attending games again, so that's what I did! The only real issue now was that I didn't have anyone to actually go with, so when I got chatting to a girl at work one day and she mentioned that her boyfriend was also a Hoop, and that maybe we could meet before the game, I jumped at the chance. From hereon, I went to matches with Leigh, and his brother Graham, and this is where the banter and making a day of it really started to take shape. The lads liked a drink – I wasn't that fussed, but welcomed the company and was happy to drive us all around the country as 'Fred Cabs' to watch the R's. We went to some great haunts, pretty much all of which were 'up north', the furthest being when Graham and I travelled to Blackburn for a resounding 1-0 defeat, a certain Mr. Shearer scoring the solitary goal.

On another occasion, Graham and I went to the Midlands to see Rangers play Aston Villa, and in the days before Sat Nag, we found ourselves just a few miles from Villa Park, and, seeing a car in front with a mini replica Villa top and scarf attached to the back window, decided to follow the chap to the ground, as clearly he had local knowledge and could no doubt steer us clear of any traffic. The circuitous route he meandered demonstrated beyond doubt the fellow knew the area well, as we trailed up and down side streets, eventually coming to a halt at a garage, where the driver pulled in and was, it transpired, taking his car in for some work. We were now stuck miles from anywhere, with no clue how to get out of the estate we found ourselves in, let alone where the hell the ground was. As is often the case with following Rangers, we would have been better staying put, as we were battered 4-1. It is the only time I have left the ground a few minutes early, trailing 3-1, to miss the ignominy of conceding another goal. The thought of seeing Villa score again was too much to contemplate and we beat a hasty exit, but were left in no doubt that we had conceded again when an almighty roar went up from inside Villa Park.

Contrary to how it may seem, I have never understood the need for people to leave a game early. Some would say they want to miss the traffic. May I suggest to these people you could save yourself a few notes and a couple of levels on your systolic blood pressure count by staying at home. How anyone can leave a game, often at 1-0 or even 0-0 is beyond me. I'm sure that dads aren't really racing home early so that they can watch *The Cube*. And what effect does it have on their poor children? They would be mentally scarred for life if forced to leave at half time 4-0 down (a la Newcastle at home), only to miss the greatest fight back in living history!

Then there was the time when I took leave of my senses (a common failing of the football fanatic) and convinced Simon, a friend of mine in Luton, who over time made the occasional trip to a game, thus becoming an 'honorary Hoop', to accompany me up the M1 after work to see our League Cup game at Sheffield Wednesday. Arriving twenty minutes late in the Steel City, we literally abandoned my Ford Escort under a nearby bridge and hot-footed it to the ground. I raced in and was bounding up the concrete steps, almost at the top before I turned round to discover Simon was nowhere to be seen. Cursing, as we'd already missed about twenty-five minutes by now, I made my way back to the turnstiles, to witness him being quizzed by the gatemen and having his pockets checked. It turned out that Simon, a keen fisherman, had fishing wire in his pocket and there was no way he was being let in, as the prospect of watching Rangers after a one hundred and sixty mile trip straight from work, having devoured only

Sainsbury's own sausage rolls, original *Pringles* and a half a bag of *Skittles* while in possession of wire could allow a serious bout of self-harm. He eventually pleaded insanity on the grounds of diminished responsibility (that and he was from Luton), and was finally let in WITH the fishing wire still on his person. At ninety minutes I asked him ever so nicely to garrotte me, on the back of a 4-0 drubbing and with the prospect of a further one hundred and sixty miles back to Luton with only a few *Pringles* and some bruised fruit to sustain me.

A further occasion where I wasted another precious day of life was a return to the Midlands, this time to face the Baggies of West Brom. I shan't bore you with the obvious (we lost, heavily, 4-1), but we did manage to hit the woodwork about fifteen times (OK, I exaggerated, it was only twelve) and should have won the game easily. I even overheard two home supporters discussing the game afterwards, claiming they were lucky to win, with 3-1 being a fairer reflection – not sure what game they had been watching, although looking at them it was more likely they watched it in the bar, something which, on reflection, I wished I'd done myself.

Sometimes we would meet other friends of the lads, the 'die hards', ever present home and away. Graham was certainly more into it than Leigh, who didn't attend all games, but one fellow I was introduced to was the chap they called 'Queenie'.

It's all a Blur...

Queenie and I travelled down to Cornwall to see Leigh marry Sarah. It was to be the venue for one of those moments in life I would never truly live down. I blame alcohol and Blur for the whole thing. I was just enjoying myself when *Country House* by the aforementioned artist started to play and in my inebriation I may just have put some actions to the words 'Lives in a house, a very big house in the country', the main one being to impersonate the roof that one normally finds on top of the said house, with two hands above my head in the shape of a triangle. Queenie never let me forget that moment of alcohol-induced madness.

The wisdom of wisdom teeth (or why you should never go to a match after having them removed)...

One match I recall (for all the wrong reasons, as will become apparent) was in 1993, when Rangers played Norwich. On the Saturday morning before the match I was booked in to my local dentist in Stevenage to have my wisdom teeth removed. As I didn't envisage this being too much of a trauma, I still very much planned to go to the game in the afternoon. Many so-called friends had shared with me the horrors of having such teeth extracted, but I dismissed it. Clearly in their case removal of wisdom teeth also extracted the wisdom that goes with them, so I really didn't see the problem.

The dentist, a large Nigerian gentleman with the touch of a pixie, had them out in about twenty minutes and I genuinely didn't feel a thing. I had been awake for the whole operation, with just injections to numb the pain, although was a bit surprised that his dental nurse seemed to spend more time mopping the floor of the crimson tide than attending to me. Meanwhile, the dentist seemed all too eager to climb on top of me at various moments during the procedure. Once everything was over and he was fully dressed again, I left for the match, in high spirits (well, local anaesthesia). The ground was about an hour away in the car, and I was driven by my friend Judith, a Scottish lass who clearly knew very little about football, as evidenced by her declaration that she was looking forward to seeing QPR, and may well have benefitted from anaesthesia herself between the hours of three and five.

We arrived around an hour before kick-off, and I was just starting to feel some minor discomfort from the gaping wounds in the right side of my mouth, but pressed on to the ground – about ten minutes' walk from where we had parked up, in a place that I knew gave us a reasonable chance of the car still being there on our return. By half time I was feeling somewhat rough, not only as Rangers were trailing 2-1 and had scored one of the Canaries' goals for them, but by now the injection had completely worn off and felt like someone was blowing ice-cold air into my ear through a loud hailer and straight into the gaping chasm where once my teeth had resided. By mid-way through the second half it must have been bad, as I instructed Judith to take me home, but she ignored me. She knew me well enough to know that this was merely the side effects of the anaesthesia talking, and that there was only one way you would get me from a match before the end: on a stretcher, with me yelling "THE PAIN! OH THE PAIN" while clutching my right ear.

With about ten minutes to go (before I severed my head with the blunt 'Guinness' pocket knife my dad had given me), my favourite player of all time, 'Sir' Les Ferdinand (#SirLesLege), struck the equaliser, sending all around me wild with delight, while I just stood (yes, stood, this was in the days of terracing, so I was not only in bloody agony but I had to stand for the duration as well) clutching my face in the vain hope the throbbing would stop long enough for me to be able to open my mouth and utter the words "pain killers". Mercifully the game ended 2-2 and as we made our way back to the car, I had terrible visions of it having been towed away, or left on four piles of house bricks. Thankfully neither was true and thus started the agony in earnest that was to continue for three days – a short period of time when you consider the number of years I had followed Rangers in abject misery.

#SirLesLege…

I feel I can't let an opportunity go by to say a few words about the greatest ever player to pull on a hooped shirt in all my years of watching QPR. 'Sir' Leslie Ferdinand. Pace. Power. Aerial ability (not as in *Sky* installer). The complete player. Let down only by the fact that he is a Spurs fan. Shame.

Joe and 'Sir' Les Ferdinand

Queenie again...

Due to my now living in Letchworth and working in London, I made the most of the £2700 annual season ticket that the railways fleeced me for annually, and used it for a 'free' ride in on Saturdays, so I was now also a season ticket holder at Loftus Road. Queenie and I had become firm friends, and we both sat in the Upper Loft. Being regulars meant we got to meet other such devoted souls, and wherever there was a regular, there was a pet name! One such individual fitting the bill was 'Poodle', a name we gave this poor unfortunate woman (and not just because she had to endure Rangers every other week), but due to her somewhat tight perm. The football at times was dreadful (when we were lucky) but the banter was good, albeit almost entirely themed by me being the butt of Queenie's bald gags, and he the butt of my fat jokes. It was always good-natured though and became part and parcel of our meetings and our regular phone conversations.

Even when we moved to the other end of the Upper Loft, we quickly found nicknames for the new set of fans in the vicinity. We now had 'Rasp', so-called as he thought there was nothing better than to blow raspberries at the team when they weren't playing that well (which was often) and also 'Villa De Poulet', a chap whose cap was emblazoned with these very words and who, as far we could tell with our pidgin French, was advertising the 'House of Chicken'. We therefore ascribed his son the name 'Drumstick'. Finally, there were the 'Bubbles', a family who we believed to be of Greek persuasion.

Queenie and I spoke most weeks about the forthcoming games and it's amazing how we always knew which players should play and who should be dropped. I guess that's just part of us men feeling we have the God-given right to tell experienced managers how to do their jobs. I mean, would that work in any other walk of life? "Excuse me officer, I wouldn't arrest this man like that, I would do it this way" (sound of felon's arm snapping), or how about "Now I know I called you out for my dripping tap, but I really think you should use a washer". Yes, quite. I suppose we justify it by the fact that these guys get paid such an incredible amount of money that they should be able to take it. We, on the other hand, are mere paupers by comparison, so the least we can do is show these prima donnas how we would do it, given half the chance.

And we would 'play for the shirt'. You see it whenever a player at your club has supported the team as a boy. Try telling them that it's about the money. Wouldn't we all, given the opportunity, play for our boyhood team, for free? What it would mean to run out onto that hallowed home turf, in front of a packed and vociferous crowd, to hear your name chanted, to have a song made up about you! To look up at that scoreboard and see your name in LCD, to know it is printed in the match day programme, for prosperity. Of course, I am awakened from this fantasy, as after a few seconds everyone in the ground realises that I am indeed crap. I can't pass, I get knocked off the ball all too easily, I have no pace (never did have, even when I weighed half of what I do now. Well, actually I ran a fairly mean 100 metres, but 90 minutes of the game has more in common with a marathon than a sprint) and I have the humiliation of being the first ever player to be substituted within two and a half minutes of the game commencing. Sure, I clutch the back of my thigh as I am roundly booed off by my own fans, but we all knew I wasn't good enough to ever play football at any level other than a Saturday morning jumpers-for-goalposts kickabout at Gladstone Park.

Playing the loyalty card...

One debate Queenie and I perpetually engaged in was that of loyalty, which would see me arguing the (my) case that being loyal to the R's wasn't just about how many games you attended in a season, but manifested itself in many other ways too. Queenie always attended more games than me and knew all he had to do to wind me up was tell me that this made him more loyal. I would normally retort by pointing out that I didn't have the money to go every week; he was single and lived in the capital, but for me even home games meant around six hours of travel and a remortgage. If only I had known someone back then who could assist with such matters, someone with an aptitude for financial planning who has a wealth of experience in the increasingly difficult mortgage market. If anyone is in need of such an individual now, then please contact me by shouting very loudly.

The wider debate of course is around the definition of loyalty – what it really means to be a loyal supporter. Is it based on the number of games attended? The number of miles covered in a season? Or perhaps how much one spends over the course of a year? For many, following their team is their life, often at the expense of having a network of friends, and nearly always to the detriment of their bank balance. I dread to think how much I have spent over the years in tickets and travel alone. Add up the number of hours spent watching matches, travelling to and from grounds, and talking/analysing each game: even multiplied by minimum wage, I reckon I could have bought my house outright and still had change for an *M&S* sandwich. Hell, let's push the boat out and assume the triple pack. Even something with rocket! (Not that I have the faintest idea what the hell rocket is. But *M&S* put it in their sarnies, so it must be expensive and clearly not something I am likely to have to leave on the side of my plate in *Greggs*.)

So, what does loyalty mean to me? I guess it means sticking by your team through thick and thin, attending as and when you can, but always showing an interest and a thirst for knowledge for everything about your club. When I was younger (so much younger than today), I travelled the length and breadth of the country (and Blackburn) to see the Queens Park Rangers. Now in my forties, with family commitments and an ailing bank balance, my attendance is sporadic, but no less passionate. When Rangers score my neighbours are in absolutely no doubt as to what has just happened, although it wouldn't surprise me if one day an officer of the law came calling to check everything is alright, confiscating my knife block along the way, just to make sure.

Once a team are in your blood, there is no escaping that hook, that bond. No matter where you are or what you're doing, if you know your team are playing you simply have to know how it's going, even if you are not there in person to witness it first-hand. I know I, like many, become pre-occupied on a Saturday around two forty-five (showing my age now – just how many games these days are played on a Saturday at three o'clock?) and could happily be left alone to stew in the juices of my own purgatory until just before five.

Should one choose to take advantage of the modern piracy that is known as live streaming, your tension levels are raised at around two fifty-seven, as you desperately search for a live stream of the game. Once found, you are faced with the very real prospect of the commentary being given by a crazed Italian, with Arabic subtitles. The dilemma then is whether to stick with the picture and turn down the sound or try re-tuning to another stream. By this point the clock is rapidly approaching three and you are normally mad enough to try anything in order to get a picture AND English commentary (I use the term loosely, as it's normally an ex-Scottish international).

This should all be made possible by super-fast broadband with speeds of up to twenty megs (so if you live 'in the sticks' like me, that's about one point nine then), and when you ring your ISP to complain (who shall remain nameless, but for the purpose of this we shall call 'Ski') you are told that it's not them with the slow connection, it's the area. Area? It's bloody Norwich, not the Sahara Desert. I know my conjugal rights, and they clearly know theirs as they are shafting me nearly a hundred notes a month for the privilege of internet speeds one gear up from carrier pigeon. If things aren't bad enough, this means that the game has more stop/starts than the Norwich to London train, although it's easy to blame the connection and the stream when actually it's the Rangers players who are that slow you don't realise that you are in fact watching it 'real time'. You end up trying all manner of things just to keep the stream moving, anything from holding the cable and wrapping it around your neck (serves a second purpose then if we are getting trounced), to standing up and keeping very still or even bouncing up and down like one does when one needs a pee.

Loyalty therefore may take many forms. The one common denominator is always caring.

The rules of engagement...

Once the game is underway, especially if it's a tense one, the rules of engagement are quite simple:
1. Don't ask me questions.
2. Don't ask me for anything.
3. Leave me alone.

If we concede, the rules change thus:
1. Ask me a question and I will metaphorically rip your head off.
2. Ask me for anything and I will metaphorically rip your head off.
3. Leave me alone and your head stays metaphorically on your shoulders.

If we score but our opponents are already out of sight:
1. Ask me a question and I will talk you through the goal, mutter that it's all 'too little too late' and allow you a few seconds to move away in order to keep your metaphorical head.
2. Ask me for anything and no. 1. above applies.
3. Best you leave me alone really.

If we score and that puts us in front, the rules change again:
1. Ask me a question and you will be greeted by a beaming lunatic, probably singing 'da da da da HOOPS' very loudly, while dancing like an inebriated hyena. I will be happy to talk you through the goal in explicit detail.
2. Ask me for anything and you are likely to get it.
3. Best you bring a bottle.

If it's a win...

If we have somehow managed to win the game, then Saturday night is great. I am more than happy to push the proverbial boat out, and it's not uncommon for me to treat the whole family to a slap-up fish and chip supper or even, if we want the full three course experience, Maccy D's. And it doesn't stop there on the spend stakes, no siree. I will gladly sink a few small Irish as well, let me tell you, while dancing round the house in my 'QPR Championship Champions 2010-2011 scarf' and looking like a less stylish, overweight Roberto Mancini as I re-enact the goal(s) in my head, occasionally going up to Joe and imitating the mad Italian from the betting advert "2-1. Sixty minoots. 2-1!!!!", even if the score was something completely different. But I'm not done celebrating yet. I pick Katie up, telling her "The Hoopies WON", thus giving us the chance to play her favourite game of 'strong arm', whereby she climbs up on each arm, first the left (the weaker one), then the right (the 'strong' one and hence the name of the game 'strong arm') and I lift her up to touch the ceiling. Even now she asks me which one is the weaker as she can never remember. Joe and I have tried to play this game as well, however he is showing signs of a lad that is nearly off to high school, so both my arms seem somewhat weak when I can only just get him off the floor. As for me trying this game with Kerri. Well, let's just move on, shall we?

If it's not a win or a draw...

Hmm. I guess this falls into the territory of me being 'hard to live with'.

The following are likely to apply:
1. Tea will be prepared by me at home, preferably with ingredients that don't need to be cut up (hide the knives), boiled in water (as I may just try and jump in the pan), or oven cooked (head in).
2. Any questions you feel compelled to ask (eg. How was your day? Did you get up to much? How much wood can a woodchuck chuck if a woodchuck could chuck wood?) are likely to be answered curtly, with grunts of one syllable that leave the questioner in no doubt that the result wasn't favourable.
3. My mouth will look like, at best, a straight line. Even if you were to paint Ronald McDonald red lips on me they would likely melt off, stating that they really didn't want to be seen on someone so miserable.
4. The *Match of the Day* theme music would not be heard that evening.
5. Alcohol levels may fluctuate between one begrudged can of something cheap out of the beer fridge to a wallowing in self-pity in some own brand cheap liquor. Either way I won't be splashing the hard-earned on any booze that is likely to leave me broke along with miserable.

One wedding and no funerals...

Saturday, the seventeenth of June, the year two thousand. A day that is etched in my memory for ever more. The day when the Mills and Hartman families joined together their offspring in holy matrimony. A carefully planned event with almost strategic precision.

- The venue: The Assembly House in Norwich, a venue we chanced upon after months of scouring suitable venues, for the grandness, lavishness and the shoestring budget we had.
- The cake: which actually collapsed at one point during the preparations on the day but which I never told Kerri about for some time afterwards, for fear of her having a nervous breakdown.
- The car: owned and driven by a retired chap who even provided his own chauffeur's hat.
- The invites: nicely produced and a touch better than I could have managed on my cheap home printer.
- The table settings: where you try to ensure people of likeminded humour, age and interests sit on the same table, but invariably it means sitting them with a long lost aunt who you know will cause some ill feeling at some point during the day.
- The bridal dress: although Kerri did buy a SECOND one for good measure and no, DON'T ask.
- The pianist: a friendly chap who was a better player than I am, but certainly wouldn't have given Liberace a run for his money.
- The DJ: who we chose because his name began with an A in the *Yellow Pages* and who played just about every song from eras other than the eighties – the precise opposite of what I had requested.

Every last detail, no stone left unturned. Originally, we chose a date which clashed with a friend's big day, so even moved ours back two weeks to ensure mutual friends could attend both (and not, as the cynics may have thought, because they were more popular and we would have had nobody at ours. Come to think of it, that would have saved us thousands. Ho hum, hindsight is a wonderful thing). It was close season, so QPR wouldn't get in the way. Everything was perfect. Well almost.

Had we realised that England's clash with Germany in the Euro Championship was on the very same day as our wedding then yes, it would have been perfect. So while I didn't have to worry so much about getting score flashes for the Rangers game, the evening was somewhat fraught, as I, like most men, still need to keep abreast of the England score. Plus this was against the Germans AND was in a major Championship. By the evening, the reception was all but deserted of the male of the species – the sight of forty-odd blokes crowded round a twenty-two inch telly in the bar area is something to savour – while I was left in the main hall with forty-odd girls (why now, when I am just spliced, do I get so much female attention?) dancing to 'Agadoo'.

Mum and Dad

Our wedding night, in the bridal suite of our nearby hotel, was memorable. Watching the re-run of the match and seeing Alan Shearer score the only goal of the game certainly got my pulse racing and got me in the mood, and then it was into bed to do what any newlywed couple would do. We opened our cards, and like excited children, we shook them to see if nice crisp (or used) bank notes or cheques made out to the happy couple fell out. This raised the excitement in the room to fever pitch, and we fell, exhausted into each other's arms before falling soundly asleep. In my dream state, I imagined how it might have been oh so different if I hadn't met a girl from Norwich – 'A Fine City' (well, that's what it says on the signposts as you enter), and had in fact fallen for a girl from the wrong side of West London...

The 'Best Dressed Five-a-Side Team'

80

The moment of coming out...

It's often said it's the hardest thing to do. You have only been seeing your new girlfriend for a while, but there is that nagging doubt. You know if the relationship is to work long term, then you are going to have to broach the subject sometime.

But it's a delicate matter. What if she looks at you, full of shock, utter amazement, hurt, even disgust? What if she ends it there and then? It's not your fault after all. It's in your make up. It's a big part of who you are. You have both already uttered those three little words to each other, so surely she will understand?

You decide that tonight you will be honest with her about how you feel. It's been on your mind now for weeks. If your relationship is to ever work, then truth must come first. At all costs.

"I have something to tell you. Please don't be mad at me and please try to understand. It's kind of difficult to say it really."

"Whatever it is, we can get through this. Truly."

"OK. Well, it's like this. I've been seeing another..."

"WOMAN! You barsteward! How could you! After all we've said to each other these past few weeks! Doesn't that mean ANYTHING to you????!!!! How could you? And to think I let you..."

"NO! Not another WOMAN! I've been seeing another TEAM. I HATE Chelsea. There. I said it! I only put up with going to matches with you because I knew how important it was and got to spend more time with you."

"You mean, you haven't been seeing anyone else?"

"Of course not. I love you and only you. I would never do anything to hurt you."

"Oh I'm so relieved; I thought I'd lost you."

"No, you're stuck with me now! I'm relieved too! I've been meaning to tell you for weeks but just couldn't pluck up the courage!"

"You soppy fool! It could never be that bad anyway! Just as

long as you don't support that rabble QPR from down the road!"

"Er. Well actually, I do as it so happens."

"QPR? Quarter Pound of Rubbish? QPR, QPR, QPR, QP ah, ah, ah, ah, ah, ah, QPR... they're CRAP!"

"Well, at least one end of our ground isn't called the SHED!"

"And what's wrong with the Shed?"

"What's RIGHT with it? And those Neanderthal fans of yours!"

"Well at least we don't have Spark the stadium cat as our mascot!"

"No, you have Stamford the pussy instead!"

"Well, I think we should split up."

"I agree."

The following morning, after I recounted my terrible nightmare to Kerri, we made use of the excellent shower room, where the shower was like a car jet wash. I sat on one of the two toilets, reading the hotel's pamphlet on 'Things To See And Do In Norwich' and parting with yesterday's excellent wedding breakfast, while Kerri took a shower. She was actually able to soak me from six feet away, such was the intensity of those jet streams.

I retell this tale not for any kind of salacious titillation, you understand, but merely because I can.

A Joe is born...

Captain's Log. Star date July 25th, 2001.

And so like an expectant father, I pace the floor, for once the analogy totally apt. Kerri has been in labour for about nine hours…

Early in proceedings I nipped outside to check on how Rangers were doing in a pre-season friendly, via Queenie. Now I wouldn't normally have been that bothered about a match that had no significance and especially on the day when my first born was due to make an appearance, but this was against Chelsea, and besides, Kerri wasn't even breathing funny yet and the woman in the next room sounded like either she was being strangled or her partner was using the old coitus interruptus method to expedite delivery, although why he would interruptus and not just coitus is anyone's guess, as clearly I wasn't in the room with them and clearly I am using Latin words to sound educated.

After getting off the phone from HRH I called Mum and Dad, to let them know that today was likely to be the day that they became grandparents. While the importance of the day was never underestimated, Mum did manage to inform me that we were 3-1 up, and for a few moments at least, the enormity of the day that was unfolding was forgotten by the equally important fact that QPR were beating hated local rivals Chelsea, albeit in a normally meaningless friendly, but this was Chelsea, so the words 'meaningless' and 'friendly' didn't apply.

Once back into the salubrious surroundings of the Lister Hospital, Stevenage's premier nightspot, and a further eight hours of labour, which saw Kerri change from the woman I married into Linda Blair's stand in double in *The Exorcist*, and after several unsuccessful efforts to get baby Joe out, the doctors opted for a 'cut and shut', or in their parlance, an emergency caesarean. Now, whenever the word 'emergency' is mentioned, one can't help thinking that things are pretty serious. And when I was told to go and change into a gown and gloves I started to get rather anxious, largely as I didn't really like the cut of the gown and the gloves didn't really suit either. Kerri was beyond the stage of calling me all the names under the sun or gripping my hand until bones started to splinter, and Joe was ready to leave the relative luxury of his bachelor pad and enter the big wide world.

Kerri was injected with a legal drug and I was asked if I could manage the simple task of holding my wife's hand, which I nodded I could, but in truth I was overawed by the occasion and the speed with which people now seemed to be running around. Had the option been there, I would have taken a shot of gas and air and a quick half of epidural myself. However, within seconds of the screen going up and Kerri's medication finally kicking in, Joseph David Hartman was out, crying at the loss of his warm inner sanctuary and allowing his dad the chance to reciprocate his tears, in that once in a lifetime moment of welcoming his first born son into the world. Joe was weighed, tagged, checked and fussed over by an entourage of doctors, nurses and registrars, while I went outside to make the calls to the world's newest grandparents, firstly the mother-in-law, then my own parents, who I knew would be waiting up anxiously for the news that would make their lives complete. I remember telling Mum first, as she answered the phone, and she was almost overcome with emotion, then put my dad on. I could actually feel the pride down the phone, all the way from Norwich.

To say Joe was a difficult baby would be like saying that those on board the Titanic may have got slightly wet when it sank. Kerri and I didn't really sleep for about nine months, baby Joe having the inability to 'sick up', so effectively he cried when his bottle was due, then cried for some three hours afterwards due to trapped wind, before starting crying again because he was hungry for another bottle. If you can imagine this cycle over and over and over again (only keep saying over and over until you pass out) you should just about be able to comprehend a millionth of what we were going through.

Queenie actually named him 'Freddie Lungsberg', as even from the safe distance of 'The Smoke', he was near deafened when calling up to talk everything Hoops. It didn't help either that we lived a hundred miles from family who could have at least shared the burden occasionally. Add to this that the 2000-2001 season was to see us relegated on forty points, to say the year was mixed would be the proverbial understatement.

Pop

My dad had a competitive streak that surfaced most when we played snooker or pool, regardless of whether we were playing in the local snooker hall in Norwich, or on a battered little three foot table at home. I remember once that I bought him a birthday card with a cartoon of two guys playing snooker, and one of them had a straw he was using to blow in his shots, such was the ease with which he was winning. I can't say that I was ever that cocky, although I was the better player (much to do with Dad being in his seventies by this stage, and with poor eyesight) and could come across as a little arrogant when knocking in another good break. However, Dad did sometimes 'get his eye in' as he put it, and if I was having one of those days where I couldn't hit a barn door from three feet, he did manage to win a few frames, much to my annoyance. It would be interesting to go back in time and play him in his youth, as from the many tales he would regale, it would appear he spent much of his adult life in and out of snooker halls and bars. On the basis of these stories, I'm surprised he wasn't:

1. World Snooker Champion ten years running;
2. Shot by one of the Kray twins for his extensive knowledge of their movements;
3. An amalgam of 1. and 2. above, with perhaps a said Kray shooting Dad to stop him becoming world champion for an 11th time.

My dad: the story teller. He was renowned for it. Percentage-wise you could never truly tell how much was fiction, fact, or faction, but they were entertaining. Over the years he would retell ones you had heard before, almost word for word, yet somehow you never really tired of hearing them. The mainstays of these tales were his days in London, growing up around the time the city was in the grip of the Kray twins. Dad didn't actually know the twins himself, but said he knew of them. His argument for what they did was that they only did it amongst themselves, the criminal fraternity, and wouldn't pick on those who tread a more straight and sombre path. He often witnessed acts of gangland violence in the clubs he frequented, and claimed that the only reason he himself didn't end up propping up a flyover somewhere was down to his close connections with the capital's Mafia hierarchy – that and he always kept his nose clean. He would regale us with yarns about small time crooks who had crossed the wrong paths, one of whom was battered senseless with snooker balls in a sock. Another was when he was queuing in the early hours in a club, awaiting his turn for the snooker balls and a fellow player decided it would be a good idea to push in the queue. The man Dad was with was clearly not one to be queue-jumped, and went up to the miscreant, reminded him that he was pushing in line, and just to reiterate that it wasn't a good idea, lifted him into the air with one hand. On returning the gentleman to *terra firma*, his legs gave way under fright, and he collapsed on the floor.

The story Dad told most often however, was a grim incident when he was in a restaurant, sitting with a friend awaiting their meal. A man on a nearby table was doing the very same thing, when in walked two other men, and in one fell swoop, lopped off the man's ear with an open razor, in front of the shocked assembled diners. Dad said he could still hear the man screaming in agony as his assailants made a sharp exit, leaving the severed appendage as a none too appetising starter on the plate in front of him.

Dad wasn't exactly what you would call an academic either. He cited his achievements at school as actually making it through the front door, before nipping out the back and off to play truant. He left school as soon as he was legally able, and worked anywhere to make a few 'bob'. He pumped petrol, but was paid a pittance by the owner, with the constant promise of a raise that he never seemed to get around to paying. Dad reminded him of this frequently, until one day his boss relented and gave him an extra shilling. Dad was so disgusted at the magnitude of the raise he had waited so long for, he simply slammed the extra money down on his boss's desk and shouted "You can't afford me, I QUIT!". He was always a radical; he never liked to be told what to do and always stood up for what he believed in. He was also quick-witted. Some years later when he was working as production manager for his father's pleating business, one of their main accounts was giving the business a particularly tough time with regards expectations on an order. Dad had heard enough and said to the client "Do you know, if you weren't one of our main accounts I would tell you to go f*** yourself. However, as you ARE one of our main accounts, I won't." That was Dad; he would always try to use his wit as opposed his fists, although he did box in his younger days, but decided to give it up, as 'getting hit wasn't his thing'.

He also had the ability to strike up a conversation with anyone. His normal greeting was a firm handshake and a salutation of 'How do you do?', invariably shortened to 'Ow do?' when greeting those that knew him best. Whilst he was one of the most generous people I have ever met, be it with time or literally the last few pence in his pocket, he was also no fool, and had all too often helped out others in the past for little or no thanks. Whenever I was asked to assist with some task or other at work, he'd say "Never volunteer for a Christmas Club". I don't think I ever fully appreciated its significance until later in life, where the words 'Christmas Club' could effectively be replaced with any event where helping out reaps no rewards and precious little thanks in return. Perhaps his greatest words of wisdom, and probably those to live your life by were "always be humble". In a world where being first, being better, being quicker, being richer and just, well, being seems high on so many people's personal agendas, it is always sobering to think back to those three little words and realise that not everyone judges success on size of achievement and being first.

Dad was always there for me when I was growing up. He maintained that "I don't care what you do with your life son, you could be a burglar for all I care, just as long as you are happy doing it". I think I got the sentiment even at a young age, although I suspect he wouldn't have been too happy having to come to Wormwood Scrubs for a weekly visit if I had pursued his suggested profession and not exactly been a success at it. I can't imagine having to sit opposite him and for him to say "Now when I said burglar, I was just giving you an example!".

He worked hard as a mini cab driver/private chauffeur, often working long sixteen hour days to help us make ends meet. He had looked after his own father for many years through ill health, but a cruel twist of fate was to change the course of his life, when his father, at the ripe old age of eighty-seven, married his live-in housekeeper. Within six months he had passed away, leaving his entire estate to his much younger bride. My grandfather had died intestate, and Dad, feeling he had a right to at least a proportion of his late father's inheritance, particularly as he had nursed him for many years before the arrival of his housekeeper, took the case to Crown Court, and after a debilitating ten years, on to High Court. The outcome was to fall in the favour of his stepmother, who retained the entire estate, including the property, which was converted into numerous flats, and even back then in the late seventies, worth around £100k.

I don't believe Dad ever recovered from that fight, indeed with the combination of financial worry, his long working hours, the need to care for me and my mother and the court case, he suffered a mild heart attack in his late fifties. I remember going in the back of the ambulance with him and my mum and how scared I was that we might lose him. Fortunately it was just a warning for him to slow down, which he did: it was the catalyst for retirement to Norfolk a few years later.

Wherever I was concerned, he always put me and my mother first. I can even recall a time when he asked his employer for a few hours off to attend my school sports day. Unfortunately they weren't so understanding and declined his request. Dad being Dad, he told them to stick their job where the sun didn't shine and walked out, then attended the said event. When I started work, he was always telling me not to put up with the treatment of some of the managers I had, but I would tread a lot more carefully and he never understood why. "Tell them to stick their job", he'd say. He couldn't appreciate that in my era it was much harder to get work and that telling managers to stick jobs every time the going got a little tough just wasn't feasible – a far cry from how things were for him back in the day.

I was very proud that Kerri and I could give him a grandson to cap his eventful life off. Dad idolised Joe and had he been a lot younger, I'm sure they would have spent many happy days together. He saw Joe's first birthday, but at the grand old age of eighty-seven, his health was failing. He became bedridden, with my mother looking after him round the clock. Kerri and I had planned a trip to North Yorkshire for a long weekend, a journey of some five hours. It was only our second day there when my mother called to say that Dad had gone.

"What do you mean, gone?" I said.

"He's dead," she said, almost matter of factly.

"How do you know for sure? Has the doctor been out?"

"Yes, he's been. Can you come home?"

I was in total shock. All I wanted to do was to hug my Joe, and I did, looking out of the window to the imposing Skipton hills.

My friend Ian was good enough to drive us back to Norwich and on arrival, I entered my parents' mobile home. There was Dad, lying still, and the enormity of it finally hit me. I broke down. Mum was calm.

"There he is," she said. "Give him a kiss. His last word was 'Frederick' as he then lay back on the bed and passed away peacefully."

Once I had composed myself, my thoughts turned to the gold cygnet ring he wore on his little finger. I asked Mum where it was as he wasn't wearing it, but she had already removed it. It was then down to me, the man of the house, to contact the funeral home and for them to come and pick Dad up and take him to the Chapel of Rest. A few days later I made the decision to visit him there, as I wasn't coping at all with the loss and my mum was keen for me to draw a line under the whole proceedings. Dad was dressed in his best suit and although I knew his body had been prepared in readiness for its final journey, I just couldn't believe how well he looked: at peace and like he was ten years younger.

By this time I had crawled into a whisky bottle and didn't intend coming out, so Kerri had to cope with me and a young Joe, as life invariably carries on. I just didn't know who I would go to now to talk to about things, although my rational side knew Dad had served his time, had left no stones unturned, and achieved everything he could ever have wanted. It was some ten days before his cremation, the longest ten days of my life up to that point, and I grieved and I drank and I sank to an all-time low. In my self-pity I was not only neglecting my family, but hadn't even noticed the effect it was having on my mum. She had lost the man she had been married to for over thirty years and I was no longer acting like the son she was always proud of, too caught up in my own troubles. I would sit at my computer and watch endless slide shows of photos of my dad with Joe, hating the fact that my son would never see what a fine granddad he had, crying almost uncontrollably at times as I sank neat scotch straight from the bottle.

I was intoxicated for most of the day and clearly, on reflection, this was the point when my drinking began to get out of control. I justified the alcohol on the basis that I had suffered a terrible loss. Mum kept her council and was surprisingly calm – too calm I felt, as she was a teetotaller, having suffered at the hands of her abusive alcoholic father as a child, watching her own mother endure drunken beatings. She never begrudged either myself or my dad a drink, indeed she openly encouraged it whenever I would visit, seeing it as a nice bonding moment, when Dad and I would have a beer or a drop of scotch together. He always made a point of having a few bottles of spirits in his cabinet, as well as a few cans of beer in the fridge, and loved to pour a drink for anyone who might pop round to see them.

We had decided on a Humanist ceremony: as Dad was a non-practicing Jew and Mum was Christian, I couldn't see a better way of doing it. The Humanist way is more a celebration of someone's life, rather than focusing on the religious aspect of it. We had a visit from a lovely lady who sat down with us and got us to talk about Dad. While you relay the story of the deceased's life, her job is to go and turn that into a summary of the many hours' worth of material you end up giving her. I actually found the process quite cathartic, as it gave the chance to tell Dad's potted history and allowed me to go over his life again. After a frosty start (typical of my mum: until she was comfortable with something/someone, she could be very harsh at the outset), Mum was happy for us to go down this route too, and she began chipping in with her own memories. She also chose the music: Frank Sinatra's *My Way*, as she felt that's exactly how Dad had lived his life.

The ceremony was a quiet family and friends affair at St. Faith's Crematorium in Norwich, only a few minutes from where they lived, with his internment a few weeks later, where both Mum and I scattered him under a lovely tree in the crematorium's grounds. I was reminded of something Dad had always said, when reading the obituaries, or if a neighbour had told him about someone passing away.

"Well, while I keep reading or hearing about people, I must still be here!"

I knew life would never be quite the same again, but I did start to return to my normal self fairly quickly, through a combination of having to look after my own family as well as my mum, and my realism telling me that Dad had achieved everything he could ever have wanted to and wasn't leaving 'short-changed'. He had passed away at the very same age as his own father and it has crossed my mind on more than one occasion that this is when I will go also. Perhaps that's why I take more risks than I should, almost the 'cat with nine lives' theory.

2002-2003 and the night the roof came off...

Rangers started to pull themselves back from obscurity in the 2002-2003 season, largely due to the togetherness and honesty that Ian Holloway, a former Rangers player and reasonably successful lower league manager, brought to the club. The season ended with Rangers in a two legged semi-final against Oldham Athletic. After a 1-1 draw away, they came back to a packed Loftus Road for a tense second leg. The game was heading for extra time when a hopeful ball out of defence by Clarke Carlisle was pounced upon by Rangers 'legend in waiting' Paul Furlong, who shook off the attentions of then Oldham defender Fitz Hall (now there's an irony!) to score into the School End after 82 minutes. The ground went absolutely bonkers, and to this day, the atmosphere generated at that moment was the greatest I have ever experienced, in spite of the twenty-odd years I had been attending Loftus Road.

It wasn't so much the goal but what it signified for so many. We were just minutes away from attending a major final for the first time in nearly seventeen years, but it also symbolised the changing fortunes of a club that had been on the brink of extinction. The last eight minutes seemed like the proverbial lifetime, with Oldham understandably throwing everything at us, and only a brilliant save by Chris Day ensured the score stayed at 1-0. On the final whistle, the place erupted into incredible scenes of euphoria. People invaded the pitch; players strutted around the hallowed turf, as did Holloway, hugely proud of what he had achieved. I called Mum and could barely hear her over the almost deafening singing from the ecstatic masses. The crowd sang "Hi Ho Silver Lining" and in that singular moment, it all made sense: why you support your team through all the bad times, the defeats, the endless miles and the sometimes seemingly thankless task of remaining dedicated.

Ask any fan what they want each week and it's not trophies (although some silverware would be nice from time to time).

It's not about league titles. It's about the players pulling on the shirt of the club you love and playing like it means to them what it does to those fans, the ones who support you week in and week out. Players come and go, sometimes because they're just not right or are happy to move on; still others outgrow you and move onto bigger and better clubs (and more money of course). But fans don't. Their life sentence is a labour of love, meaning that when match day comes around (which can be any day at all these days, including a Thursday night, if in some strange European competition), you have no option but to find a radio or television, glue yourself to your mobile for a friend's text message or just to be there so you can see how the next episode pans out in the longest, never-ending soap opera of football.

We love you Bircham...

One player who epitomised what it meant to be a fan and the relevance of pulling on the sacred Hooped shirt at the time was Marc Bircham, a lifelong Hoop who really did live the dream and play for his beloved Rangers. That season he had helped us to within the brink of a return to the First Division with his marauding performances from centre midfield, and this colourful character really did let the season go to his head (literally) by dying his hair blue and white. This was the man who would reveal his replica Guinness top from the mid eighties under his match day shirt whenever he scored, emblazoned with 'Birchams 8 Chelsea' on the reverse. Fans loved him because we knew for him it felt just like any one of us playing for our team. The Frankie Valli song *You're Just Too Good To Be True* also got the Rangers fans singing along with the words: 'We love you Bircham, because you got blue hair, we love you Bircham, because you're everywhere, we love you Bircham, Rangers through and through'.

I often tried to imagine what it would be like to be Bircham and actually play for the club you supported. How many of us have imagined stepping out onto the hallowed turf of our favourite club and receiving a pass in the 90th minute of an ever so important game, deadlocked at 1-1 and destined for a draw, and smashing it into the top corner, thus winning the game 2-1!

"YYYYYYYYYEEEEEESSSSSSSSS!!!!!!!! (adopting mock Italian accent) 2-1! 2-1! 90 minoots! 2-1!"

Well, I have always known my lack of genuine ability, in collaboration with me not being the sveltest of creatures, would mean I was destined to be a follower rather than a player. Then along comes baby son, and we suddenly transfer all of those feelings onto him, that one day he too could be waiting in the wings for his chance, with the scores locked at 1-1.

"And Rangers are making a substitute. Off comes some vastly overpaid foreign import who is merely collecting his £80 large a week with no intention of playing for the shirt. On in his place, and making his debut for the R's, it's number 10 Joe Hartman!"

I'm straight on my feet to applaud my son as he enters the field of play. It's not easy doing a 'Gavin Peacock' (a clap over the head) while trying to call your other half at the same time. I get on the phone to Kerri.

"It's Joe, he's just come on for his debut!"

And there he is. Would he remember all those things I told him? When we used to play out in the park in front of our house? "Head over the ball. SHOOT! Get your laces through it! Nibble him! That's it, use your strength!" I am brought back to earth as Rangers have a free kick just outside the box. I look over at the scoreboard and it's 89 minutes, just like I remember it in my dream. The referee's shrill whistle brings us all back to the moment, as the ball is played sideways and there, running onto it, is Joe. The crowd seem to suck everything in as he lets fly from fully thirty yards. It leaves his right foot almost in slow motion, and the ball whistles into the top right hand corner. As it caresses the net there is one almighty ROAR as we take the lead!

"YYYYYYYYYEEEEEEEESSSSSSSSS!!!!!!!!"

It's in! Joe has scored the winning goal on his debut! The crowd goes wild, and I leap into the air, and on my way down I begin hugging and kissing random strangers around me, shouting:

"YES! YES! That's my son! Joe Hartman! That's my son!!!!"

As the crowd begins to settle back in their seats, I call Kerri to tell her the amazing news.

"Joe SCORED! His first touch in the game! A screamer from 35, maybe 40 yards!"

"Oh wow, well done him! It's lasagne and garlic bread tonight when you get in."

But then I am reminded of the words of my dad.

"Son, I don't mind what you do. As long as you are happy doing it."

And then it all makes sense. I don't need Joe to score the 89th minute winner for QPR and make Rangers folklore. I am just as happy looking out of the window and seeing him playing for fun with his mates. In fact, I don't need Joe to do anything other than be happy and the best he can be at whatever life path he meanders down. And I know I will always get more out of a kickabout with him and his mates than watching some prima donna strut his stuff.

The lottery of the Play Off Final...

And so to the Play Off Final itself, which saw us up against Cardiff City at the Millennium Stadium (which, for the non-geographically minded, is also in Cardiff), so effectively we were playing them at home. I travelled to the game with Big Ali and Queenie, and after making the obligatory joke that we were glad we hadn't gone about an hour into the journey and forgotten the tickets, before realising we had gone about an hour into the journey and we really had forgotten the tickets, we still arrived in plenty of time to soak up the big match atmosphere, albeit that we arrived around lunchtime and the city was somewhat deserted, other than the advanced party from West London, keen to make an early impression. Some 30,000 were expected to be cheering on the Londoners, the biggest turnout since our Milk Cup Final defeat in 1986. As three o'clock edged closer, the city came alive and the mass of noise and colours outside the ground was amazing. This continued into the hugely impressive stadium, which, by kick-off, filled with 66,000 spectators, all eager to see the culmination of a gruelling season, but more importantly a place back in the First Division – just one division away from being back in the big time.

As the players entered the arena, it really was hairs on the back of your neck stuff (if I was being greedy, hairs on the top of my head would have been nicer). Rangers played in a change strip of white, with shirts especially made for the day, a homage to the 1967 kit that saw us win our only ever trophy against West Bromwich Albion. All Rangers fans would be hoping for a repeat of that result. The game got underway, and as expected, was a tense affair, with the whole season riding on this one match. At ninety minutes there were no goals and little between the teams, so extra time would next aim to determine who booked the dream ticket. With just a few minutes remaining and penalties now a distinct probability, Cardiff played a hopeful ball over the top of the R's stretched defence, and substitute Andy Campbell wrote himself into Cardiff folklore by lobbing Chris Day and scoring the decisive (only) goal of the game. The other half of the ground erupted, while we were left only to wonder what might have been, if, for instance, Tommy Williams had made the far more obvious pass (well, to us up in the gods) to an unmarked Furlong instead of taking the shot himself. As the whistle went, we all just stood there, in the bitter realisation that we would be spending another season in Division Two.

'The Three Amigos'

It wasn't long, however, before that disappointment was replaced with a sense of immense pride. Yes we hadn't made it – this time. But there really was a feeling that next season would be ours. We had the players. We had the manager. We had the fans. Most of all we had belief, momentum and the PRIDE back, something of course typified by Bircham, who along with fellow supporter and striker Kevin Gallen, cut particularly forlorn figures at the end of the match, especially the former, in tears but still resplendent in blue and white striped hair. As we traipsed away from the ground, I was on the phone to my mum, who had listened to the match on the elephant radio.

"Never mind mate," she said.

"It's alright mum, we played well, just wasn't to be our day. But we will be back."

I genuinely believed we had turned the corner and that 'our day' wasn't far off.

2003-2004 and every cloud has a silver lining...

The following season we picked up where we had left off and continued to play with the spirit that Holloway had now instilled in the side. There was a belief growing among all supporters that we could really do it this time. We got off to a great start, dispatching Blackpool 5-0 at Loftus Road, which I attended and not surprisingly lapped up in the bright August sunshine. We then went on to win four of our first six matches in August, losing just once. We were unbeaten in September and by Christmas had won another nine games. Plymouth were our main rivals that season and after beating them in November we led the table.

With Christmas just a month away, Kerri and I were doing the annual pilgrimage to the garden centre with a young Joe in tow, trawling through all manner of decorations. I called Mum as usual, like I did pretty much every day, to see how things were, but when I got no response, I became concerned. This was most unlike her. I tried again a while later and still nothing, so I told Kerri that we had to get over to her and see what was happening. I found her slumped on the sofa in her small mobile home, awake, but with her speech badly affected. I knew instantly she had suffered a stroke and called an ambulance, waiting with her until they arrived. She was driven away to the Norfolk and Norwich hospital, where she was made comfortable.

Coincidentally I bumped into an old school friend, Jon, who was now a GP and working at the hospital, and he came and visited my mum on several occasions. Her consultant said he was happy with Mum's progress, and even felt she could make a full recovery over time.

I visited her every day throughout December, but it was a difficult time, what with me just having started a new job as a sales manager, Christmas just around the corner and seeing Mum clearly in distress. Her speech was extremely poor, her mobility almost non-existent. She desperately tried to get me to do things for her by writing down instructions for me on paper, which included paying her papers, her rent and cancelling her milk delivery! The saddest time was when she wrote that she 'had been to hell and back' on a notepad, one that I had used to write down scores of the R's games for her. I really wanted to give her the pick up of seeing Joe, whom she idolised, but also knew that for him to see his 'Nanny Lolly' like that – it wasn't the way a small child should see her.

A difficult Christmas came and went and Mum was to be moved to a convalescing home just outside of Norwich. This brought some renewed hope that she was well enough, at least, to be moved from the more intensive care of the main hospital. It certainly meant we could go into 2004 in slightly better spirits. However, this new-found optimism was short-lived, as shortly after Mum's intake, they sat me down and told me that her condition would never improve; her speech and movement were unlikely to ever return. The day after New Year's Day, Liz, a very old friend of Mum's and former neighbour of ours from our days in Neasden, paid her a visit, travelling up from Bishop's Stortford. While Mum didn't seem in the best of spirits that day, she knew Liz was there, and it was nice that she could see her friend and in turn, good of Liz to make the long trip to see her. We both left to allow Mum to get the rest she needed, with my mind in a whirl as to what was to become of her in the short, medium and long term with regards living and care arrangements.

She's out of my life...

The call, when it came, was in the early hours of the morning on January 3rd, 2004. As anyone who has ever received a call when in a deep sleep knows, you kind of jump up and just try to stop the ringing as soon as possible, so as not to wake up the rest of the house and half the street.

"Mr. Hartman?"

"Yes, it is."

"Hello there, its Aylsham Hospital here. I'm afraid I have some bad news for you."

"OK."

"It's your mother. She sadly passed away a short time ago."

Mum had lost her relatively short battle with the after-effects of her stroke. I can't begin to write the feelings that went through me when the call came in from the hospital where she was supposed to be recuperating. Unlike my dad, who was eighty-seven and had lived his life to the full, I always felt short-changed with Mum, at a mere seventy-two. Indeed, she was still looking after Joe (a fully fledged toddler at this time) on a Thursday afternoon, to allow Kerri to go to work.

There really isn't anything you can say at this point. Kerri had awoken and could easily guess what was being said.

"I'm terribly sorry, we just thought we should let you know as soon as possible."

"Yes, you did the right thing, thank you for letting me know."

I remember putting the phone down and looking at Kerri.

"She's gone."

I remember getting up and us going downstairs for a stiff drink. I don't remember too much more.

The following day I was sitting in my toilet when Joe came in and saw me, crying.

"Nanny Lolly?" he asked.

"Yes."

"Gone to see the angels?"

"Yes."

I covered my face in my t-shirt and cried uncontrollably while he hugged me. How he knew I don't know.

Two days later I returned to work – a huge mistake as it turned out, and one that was the catalyst for much worse times ahead for me in the days, weeks, months and even years to come. I tried to be all 'British' about it, stiff upper lip, to hide my feelings this time around, as I didn't want to sink into a bottle again and try and block it all out, like I had done with my dad. This time it was about trying to work through it. I had Kerri, and Joe, and this time I would cope better. I visited Mum in the Chapel of Rest: unlike my dad, who looked at peace and genuinely ten years younger, Mum seemed to have taken Dad's years and genuinely looked like someone who had battled her stroke but eventually succumbed to it.

Her cremation was also to be at St. Faith's Crematorium, like my dad's, not far from where they lived. We had arranged for the wake afterwards to be at a local pub and in honour of mum's favourite food: fish and chips. Everyone sat around and ate the very same meal in homage to her. It was truly the saddest day of my life and I was so thankful when it was over, so that I could move on with my own life. What I didn't realise was that I never truly grieved for her, and slowly this was to have an adverse effect on my life, relationships and actions. I'm told I drank more (although I don't really remember) and I struggled with my new role as a regional manager for a retail bank, becoming increasingly intolerant of anything and everything. I became a person that I really didn't want to be. I visited the place where my parents' ashes were scattered over and again, hoping that I would find answers in the pretty gardens of the crematorium, but sadly I didn't. I felt lonely, like I was truly alone and yet I had wonderful friends around me as well as a great family, but I pushed them away and to this day I am truly sorry for that.

She would have been a wonderfully eccentric grandmother to the kids, with her gruff London ways and her unique turn of phrase. I miss her honesty, her bluntness, her legendary fry-ups. I miss having someone who was always there, who always supported me no matter what, who saw every little thing I did as an achievement, who literally would give the last penny she had. I miss her home accounting, where piles of money were allotted to the gas, water and electric bills respectively, as well as her catalogue, which allowed her to buy Joe amazing Christmas presents far beyond her means otherwise. I miss not having to go around Norwich city shops, trying to find a ceramic robin she didn't have, or a bell, or a thimble or even an elephant, all of those things she collected over the years. I often joked that if I could find a robin riding on an elephant's back, while ringing a bell with a thimble on its head, I would have finally cracked it!

I miss not being able to call her every day, sometimes twice and more often than not to talk about nothing in particular. I especially miss not being able to call her after a match, to talk her through the performance (and hopefully a few goals), as I knew she wouldn't have learned much from *Five Live* on her blue elephant radio (down to the fact that they needed to cover too many games to really give us much air time). I miss the scrapbooks she lovingly created season after season, with newspaper cuttings from all our games, and which she would decorate with blue and white tissue paper or a cut-up carrier bag from the club shop. I miss her sneezing twenty times (although I think between them my kids might have picked up that gene) and my dad telling her to "pack it in".

But most of all I miss her, because as with all mums, she was a one off, the best you could ever have, and I loved her with all my heart. I still miss her to this day and know I always will, no matter what.

I have likened the experience of losing a loved one, and the time it takes to recover even to a point of acceptance, as a bit like being a recovering alcoholic. Every day without drink is a triumph, rather like getting through every day without that person. Just being able to function without breaking down or wanting to spend the day in bed alone is a victory in itself. The recovering alcoholic knows he or she is just a day away from having another drink and losing sobriety again. In much the same way, losing a loved one means you are always a memory, a birthday, a song or a saying away from being painfully reminded that the person is no longer there. They say that time heals all wounds, and it is true that over time the loss does soften, as the good memories somehow envelope the bad ones and put some perspective on everything.

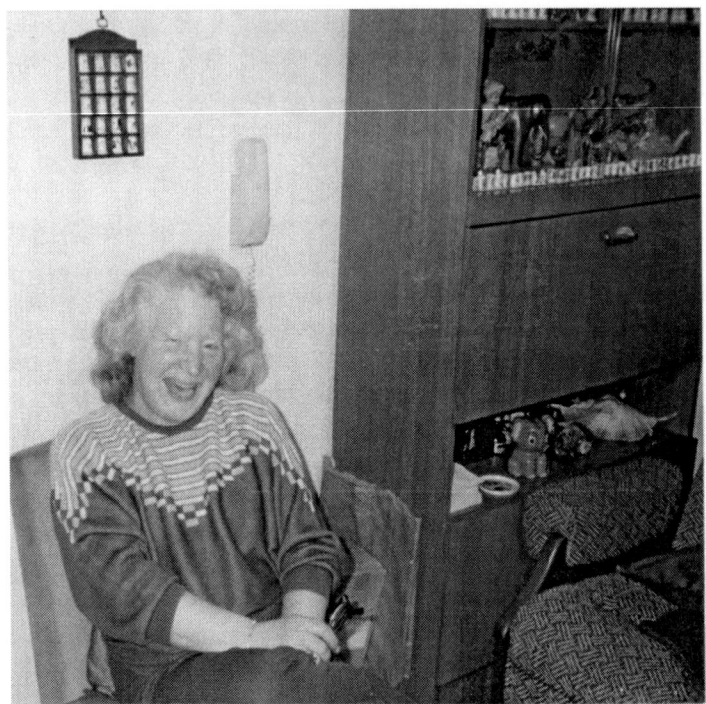

Mum and blue elephant radio

The next few months were a blur as I tried to come to terms with the loss of my mother, trying to be a father and a husband, while still relatively new in my sales manager job. I remember back to one time I went to call my mum and Kerri asked me what I was doing.

"Calling Mum," I said.

"But she's been gone months."

Rangers continued to fight to get out of the Second Division, and by the time the season was drawing to a close we still had a chance of winning the title, although our hopes rested on beating Plymouth in their own back yard. However, it was the Pilgrims who ran out 2-0 winners and in so doing secured the title for themselves. Now we were playing for runners up spot, which would of course still see us back to the First Division.

Next up, and the penultimate game of the season, we were up against Swindon. A nervous and packed Loftus Road knew that a win here would mean that we went to the last game of the season, where a win would seal promotion. Within minutes, the R's took the lead through Martin Rowlands, and the crowd (me swelling the already swollen ranks that day by one) went ballistic! The goal calmed the players in the fever pitch atmosphere, but we still had 88 minutes left to hang on! And hang on we did!

Our fate would now be sealed at Hillsborough, home of Sheffield Wednesday, a ground steeped in tradition and sadness. The question was: would there be tears of joy or sadness in a week's time? I felt a slight lump in my throat as I looked up to the heavens and mouthed "one more" to my mum. I knew that if there was such a thing as an afterlife and if she was able to look down on me at that moment, then she knew we were close to finally achieving something after all those years.

Hillsborough and the Steel City...

So, to the big day. My second trip to Hillsborough, and hopefully with a better outcome than the last. Queenie and I set off for what we both hoped would be a great day, with plenty of banter in the car to steady the nerves, then a meet up with my friend Ian in Sheffield. The R's fans were buzzing, with it all to play for, while the Sheffield mob were ambivalent, having watched their side struggle all season. Some seven thousand travelling R's packed in behind the goal to watch our side try to make history. As the players came out, the balloons were cast high into the Sheffield sky and the roar told us that it was show time!

Again, an amazingly tense game commenced, with Wednesday taking every opportunity to try and spoil our day. After 15 minutes, their tannoy announcer even updated everyone that Bristol City (our closest rivals, who could still mathematically catch and overtake us if we slipped up) were winning 1-0! Their fans loved it and started to goad us from within their pen, with R's fans only a matter of feet away. Then as the half wore on, R's legend Kevin Gallen put us 1-0 up and sent us absolutely berserk! I was sitting with Ian, while Queenie was elsewhere, as we hadn't been able to get tickets together. While it was good having Ian, a Gooner, with me, I regret not sitting with Queenie, as it just seemed fitting that we should watch this one out together, having been side by side through much of the rollercoaster ride of previous troubled years.

Half time: Rangers were kicking towards us in the second half. We opened brightly again, and were rewarded soon after the restart, when Paul Furlong controlled superbly in the box, turning and smashing a second goal home. Cue the party celebrations! The place went bonkers and we all really started to believe that this was going to be our day.

But this is Rangers we are talking about, and we never can do it the easy way! Wednesday broke clear and halved the deficit through Shaw, 1-2! They then threw everything at us, as their paltry crowd suddenly got behind their team and they really fancied it. A few more scares were endured before a mazy run down their right side by Martin Rowlands saw his teasing cross turned in by Owls defender Carr on sixty-nine minutes, and Rangers led 1-3!

Could we hold on for another twenty minutes? We just had to, it was our destiny, in our own hands. The crowd cheered the boys on as best we could, and the next thing I know I'm watching the scoreboard and see the clock click to 90 minutes. I remember Ian saying that we were there, but I still didn't dare to believe him. Not until that final whistle went would I know we had finally made it. And when it did arrive, so did my tears of absolute elation, relief, pride and sadness, all rolled into one. I looked up at the heavens, blew Mum a kiss and mouthed "That's for you and Dad". It just seemed such a fitting end to what had been a tough few years for me. Finally something tangible to really be proud of.

The celebrations were immense! Ian Holloway was chair-lifted by the players and milked the applause, Marc 'Birch' Bircham and Kevin 'Magic Hat' Gallen playing for the side they supported too and loving the day, the fans, the colours, the noise, we had done it! One step forward, after all the heartache of relegation from the Premier League and League One, administration, substandard teams, the lack of pride and passion. All forgotten there and then. All those trips, the hours of travelling and having to endure away defeats with inept performances, mismanagement of the club and its finances, all instantly dispersed. Ian and I left the stadium to meet Queenie outside, and I remember going over to him and giving him a big man hug. I knew what it meant to him too.

We walked back into town to catch the tram back to where we had parked up, packed liked sardines but we all still sang our hearts out! When Queenie and I finally got back to the car, rather than just set off, we sat, ate our sandwiches and called up a few friends, and in unison we sang on the hands free:

The R's are going up,
The R's are going up,
And now your gonna believe us,

And now your gonna believe us,
And now your gonna believe uuuussss.
The R's are going up!!!!

We decked the car out with our scarves and made our way
back south, both absolutely 'made up'. The R's were back, and
as it was to turn out, not into the First Division as we had
expected, but to a newly named league: the Championship.

The walking dead...

I do see people when I am out and somehow view them differently now, I must admit. There is an exclusive club out there that nobody ever wants to join of their own free will, of people who have lost loved ones. On bad days, it's like we are all members of the walking dead; like zombies, we pass each other by in our own world. The problem is that there are certain trigger points, maybe a song, or something someone says that reminds you of those you have lost. It's not so much a direct question that knocks you off course, as you can fend those off and (hopefully) by the nature of your reply, the person quizzing you will 'proceed with caution' or back off accordingly. What gets to me the most is when my kids say something, and Kerri will look over at me and say "that's what your mum would have said" or "that's your dad talking".

It can be actions and mannerisms as well, such as my mum's habit of sneezing and not being able to stop for about 15 sneezes, at which point my dad would offer his "turn it in will you love, for Christ's sake!". It's a habit my son and, in particular, my daughter seem to have adopted. Yes, I know your general practitioner will tell you that sneezing is the body's way of eliminating irritants or a foreign body from your nasal passages. Yet I seek comfort, however small, in the fact that it is a facet of my dear late mother that she passed on, just as my dad passed his baldness and cuddliness on to me! I think my sense of humour and personality were an amalgam of them both, as well as their low tolerance levels and ability to cut you out of their lives if felt genuinely let down in some way, not that this is necessarily the best trait to adopt, as people should, in most cases be given a second chance, but one nonetheless that is directly descended from them.

It's funny, how when you really need to speak to someone they are not there anymore. Grief hits us at any time, and there are many things I have written over the years that I don't remember writing. Whole passages of my life are missing, as if someone has ripped out the pages from the diary and burned them. You question your faith (or lack of it), you look for reasons and rationales as to why it happened, and the timing of when it did. You look to justify why people pass away and out of your life. If only you had said the right things at the right times. But you don't get a second chance to put it right. There are no real happy endings, like in *Ghost*, where we get that final chance to say our goodbyes, and know that our loved ones are doing OK on the 'other side', or for them to check that even though we're grieving for them we too are doing OK. That's why all the clichés of 'living each day like it's your last' really do have some justification.

A Katie is born...

Katie was to be the surprise arrival, unplanned, and as I always joke, Kerri's pregnancy seemed to coincide with an increase in our doorstep milk delivery – suspicious, as we neither had a milkman nor paid for milk to be delivered. Now I come to think of it, we don't really have a doorstep either. Notwithstanding, our worst fears were that she was going to be a baby cast from the same mould as Joe, and if that were the case, I would be resigning myself to a first year sleeping rough in the shed. If we dared to dream, she would be completely the opposite, in terms of the birth itself and in being able to burp up with the minimal amount of back-patting, just like so many of our friends' babies seemed to be able to do. If we were being really greedy, maybe the odd night's sleep might be nice too.

As it happened, Kerri opted for a planned caesarean this time around, working on the premise that the trapdoor was still in place, it just needed opening again, and certainly not for the reason, as was proving with some celebs and film stars, that they were 'too posh to push'. It's strange second time around actually booking into the hospital for the procedure. It almost felt like we were booking into a hotel, only without the comfy beds and Lenny Henry telling us how 'premier' it was. So on December tenth, 2004, Kerri and I set off for the Norfolk and Norwich hospital, bag packed, and checked into our room. Everyone was relaxed, and indeed, as Kerri was wheeled through to the theatre, Christmas songs were playing on the radio and the nurse was passing round *Quality Street* like it was the works Christmas party. Kerri took a chocolate and was told she couldn't have it just yet, so I took it from her and slipped it in the top pocket of my rather splendid gown. I felt quite calm, sitting next to Kerri as she lay in readiness for the grand unveiling. It was Rangers' first season in the newly named Championship, and while we weren't tearing up any trees, we weren't in any real danger of undoing all our hard work, so seemed destined for that old adage of 'mid-table mediocrity'. Having witnessed more downs than ups in recent years, this was a place I had long craved for.

As the Christmas classics continued on the radio, I was asked if I wanted to see Katie's arrival. Now, even though I like nothing better than watching a good gory horror movie, I know these to be fake and that the alien's entry (or exit, to be precise) from John Hurt in the 1979 film of the same name is actually a glove puppet and plenty of red dye for good measure. When it comes to "would I like to see a small baby being cut from its mother's womb", my inclination is to rather wish I was somewhere else, even Craven Cottage, possibly the worst football ground I have ever had the misfortune of attending, as:

1. It's in West London and, as we all know, there is only one team from that part of the capital worth mentioning;
2. We lost;
3. Please refer to 1. or 2. above.

"Well, we will tell you when she is nearly out, so if you change your mind, you can see her then," I was politely informed by the nurse. I didn't see that I would be changing my mind anytime soon, and chomped on my hazelnut and praline whirl with some vigour.

As the procedure took place behind the screen, Kerri and I chatted, a far cry from the last time we did this and her near Oscar winning performance in *The Exorcist*. Then, as if by magic (and no, a shopkeeper didn't appear), when told that Katie was about to join us, I suddenly had an epiphany: if I don't see this it won't be repeated, as we don't intend doing this again, including the sex part (a given after four years of marriage and now having two children).

At this point I stood up, and peered over the screen, to see the amazing sight of my baby daughter looking up at me, and clinging onto her cord for the last time. Words failed me, as the sight was indeed a poignant one, and besides, I was about to collapse back in my chair under the weight of all that mixed emotion. Within seconds there was the cry to signal Katie Emily Hartman had joined us in earnest. After a brief moment of irritation for her as she was weighed and tagged, I was able to hold her, before passing her on to her proud mum, looking a lot less fraught than the last time we played this game. I left mother and baby doing well and called my mother-in-law to tell her she had a third grandchild, saving the joke of "we just need another and then you will have one of each" for another day.

It was of course with much sadness that I didn't have to make another call that day to inform proud grandparents of the new arrival, but if there was ever a moment that I felt someone was watching over us, then that was it.

Facebook does have its uses...

Facebook. Love it or hate it, most people know about it. It's another form of the so-called 'social media' and I do use it.

Yes, I did get a wee bit addicted to it and yes, I did need counselling to wean me off (I can get by on only four hours a day now, so long as I take an anti-depressant four times a day as well). The one thing that does baffle me though is the pictureless profile. Suppose you find someone on there who you believe to be a long lost 'friend' (can they really be that much of a friend if you haven't seen them for over fifty years anyway, but I digress, as is commonplace) and they don't put up a picture of themselves (so basically the default outline). You can't actually tell if it's them or not.

Surely the clue is in the title 'Facebook'? OK, I grant you: the 'book' bit is a bit misleading, as it's usually on a laptop or PC screen, but come on, I mean! 'Face'! You need a picture! Of course, if over time you actually do look like a silhouette, then fair enough. However, I have never seen anyone in town that looks like that bloody silhouette and if I did, I would walk past them, thinking "I'm sure I know that bloke from somewhere, can't be certain it's him though". I guess that's how most of Rangers backline must have felt in the late nineties.

The other rather annoying thing that some people do is to put a picture up that is:

- A picture of something else, like their labrador;
- A picture of a rock star that so clearly they are not;
- Some form of caricature.

So when I was searching for people I may know (yes, you know you do it, old girlfriends/boyfriends – assuming you can remember their names when you only met them once in a dark club and could only recognise their tonsils again), I happened upon a 'Nigel Paice', not that there were that many people on there with that name, but I didn't recognise any of them from their pictures, although it had been some twenty-five years or more since I last saw him, so for all I know he may now have been a silhouette. One picture on there was a cartoon style character. It had spiky hair. It had glasses. Eyes close together. Smart suit. It was therefore nothing like the Nigel I remembered. However, I took a chance, fired off an email and waited to see if after all those years of hurt they were about to culminate in me finding the man responsible for my longstanding abject misery.

My wait wasn't long, and incredibly the man behind the strange little cartoon WeeMee was the very same, the original, accept no substitutes, the one and only, I give you, Mr. Nigel Paice.

We exchanged numbers and as you might expect, that initial chat went on for a good three hours. A real shame, as I was paying. But we soon got the boring stuff out of the way, like the last twenty-five years, family, work, etc. and got on with the really important stuff. The Hoops.

It was just like we had never been away in many respects. And thus, just like an episode of *This Is Your Life*, we were re-united.

Saturday August 6th, 2006 - And Joe comes of age...

I wrote not long after our return from the game...

It is with some trepidation that I begin writing this. Not least that it has all been done before and by better people than me. I've not only seen *Fever Pitch*, but I have actually READ the book – and I don't read! Oh, don't get me wrong, I CAN read, got an English A level in it don't you know, and sometimes I guess it's because I was force fed ten books to enable me to pass the bloody exam that I now find my mind waning after only a few pages of anything. So it's magazine articles only for me these days. And there this morning I received nearly six hundred pages of my club's fanzine's greatest bits, compiled over nearly twenty years.

So what have I got to offer that such publications and great prose hasn't already covered in abundance in the past? Well, nothing actually. Apart from that this is me telling the story of my twenty-seven year love affair with Queens Park Rangers. And that today was special. It's the 12th August, 2006. So what? We beat Southend 2-0 to record our first win in 14 matches. Big deal! I sat in Ellerslie Road. Yea yea, seen it, done it before.

So what's special? Well, today I sat with someone very special. It was his first game EVER, his first trip to London EVER, his first trip on the underground EVER. This special person was my son Joseph, aged five. (Well, four, if the train conductor asks. I mean twenty quid for a child over five, free if he's four, I ask you!)

And what a day it was. Travelling down on the big train from Norwich, both wearing our new replica tops, meeting a Spurs fan on board who made the obligatory jokes about not supporting a proper team like he did (yea, I detected the Norwich accent mate, try supporting your own team!), meeting Ipswich fans on the train who even gave me and Joe a sweetie each (nice touch – mind you, the least they could do after slating us all the way there – hey, Tractor Boys, it's early days

I know, but we're 13th after today's result, and you are????
Bottom! Played three, won nil, drawn nil, lost three!), going on
the underground and Joseph realising that all it is really is a
series of long tunnels (good spot son!), looking out over the
Thames from Blackfriars Bridge, so we could see boats, and
buildings, and where Daddy used to work in a previous life,
and then there was the football.

We met an old pal and ex-work colleague of mine,
affectionately known as 'Big Al' before the game (no, he
really is big, twenty five stone last time of asking) and his son
Alex. Then it was the turn of 'Uncle Queen', aka HRH, outside
the box office for a quick natter, then who should appear larger
than life (well larger than a real moggy anyway), but Jude the
Stadium Cat! Cue photo opportunity for Joe and said feline
fella!

It was quite a day for me:
once in our seats, Daddy starts
to point. Up there Joe, up the
top there, is where I used to
sit with my daddy (for those
of you old enough to
remember the Upper School
End used to be for HOME
supporters!). And up there
Joe, see 'Uncle Queen'
waving? (Bless him, he waved
up at the stand but I don't
think he could actually see
Uncle Queen at all!) Joe
spotted that the players were
just warming up, and running
around cones, like he does
when he goes to football

Joe and Jude

practice. And then they went back inside "so they could put on
their Hoopie shirts!", and we heard *London Calling* ('Where
they sing on the bridge'), and the Teams arrived wearing their
Hoopie shirts, and we played well, and we SCORED!!!!!!
Martin Rowlands with a screamer! And the ground erupted

into rounds of Pigbag and 'Da da da da HOOPS! Da da da da da da da da HOOPS! And I lifted Joe up and we sang it together. It was the moment I had dreamt about, being where I am always welcome and always feel I belong, and having my son with me. Now I know what my dad must have felt like all those years ago when we used to watch, and drink soup from a flask at half time, Dad all covered up in his big scarf and his leather coat. Whichever cloud you were watching from today Dad, I bet you were proud too.

The minutes silence/applause for the late Kiyan Prince also brought it home to me just how special your kids are and how short life really is, and that life is just a series of memories like these that you make and that weave intricately together to make a lifetime.

Sadly Joe was not 100% today, so after a trip to First Aid at half time for a couple of shots of that wonder drug they call *Calpol*, he slept on me for the second half, but he didn't miss anything: no more goals, but three valuable points had been earned with Rowly's wonder goal and a first for aussie Nick Ward in the first half.

Then it was over, applause all round. Three points secured and the *Calpol* finally kicked in, as Joe was outside asking where the underground was and could he have his Maccy D for tea! We made it back to the Big Train with four minutes to spare with our Golden Arch eats safely tucked away in their bags, and we munched them en route to Norwich, Joe watching his portable DVD player and Daddy reading his programme.

So, a good day was had by all. So waddya reckon reader? You heard this all before and better, right? Wrong! You ain't heard it before, coz this is about me and my Joe, and it's not like any other love, this one is different because it's us. OK, now I'm plagiarising Marr and Morrissey, but you get the point. *Fever Pitch* is about Gooners, this is about me, my love of the Hoops, and the love of my son, which just so happened to all come together in the same place, at the same time today between 3 and 5pm, on Saturday August 12th, 2006.

Thirty Years of Hurt Never Stopped Me Dreaming...

The four seasons that followed (as in 2006-2007, 2007-2008, 2008-2009 and 2009-2010 and not the mid-sixties band or the hotel group) were largely uneventful. Well, unless you were on the management team. Then it must have been like playing Russian roulette with a gun with a bullet in each chamber. Rangers saw off no fewer than twelve in that time. I half expected them to open a new turnstile at the ground to allow the new incumbents easier access in, while allowing the exiting so-called failure to slip away. That, or have a delicatessen style ticket machine installed, so that when a number was called the new man could simply enter. No sooner was he in situ, he would hear the next number called and know his time was up.

It wasn't until the owners, in the form of Flavio Briatore and Bernie Ecclestone, finally realised that to have any chance of a long overdue return to the big time they perhaps needed to find a manager and keep him for longer than five games, while not picking the team or generally interfering each week. So, when towards the end of the 2009-2010 season they appointed Neil Warnock, the feelings within the QPR Community were mixed. Some were out and out disgusted at the appointment, while others thought he would only be there a few weeks anyway.

After staving off relegation, it was then down to Warnock to try and do what no other Rangers manager had been able to do for many years. Keep his job.

Oh, and take QPR back to the Premier League after sixteen long years.

45.00 The referee blows his whistle to end the First Half

SECOND HALF

Prologue
Pre-Season 2010-2011

Pre-season arrived, bringing with it that perennial mixture of hope, optimism, and trepidation, as it's the one time when all the teams start on zero points. You are still, however, put into a mock table and your position is decided on alphabetical standing, so Barnsley led the way from when the first tables were printed around July, much to the delight of their success-hungry fans, while Watford propped up everyone else, much to the chagrin of theirs. Clearly this table means nothing, though I couldn't help but feel a ripple of annoyance that Norwich City still sat higher than us by sheer default of having their name start three letters ahead of ours. Oh, how I sometimes wish we were taken over by Arry Aardvark, who instantly decides to rename the club after himself.

Rangers had strengthened considerably (for once), bringing in players with a mixture of experience and potential talent, ranging from Shaun Derry and Clint Hill on free transfers from Crystal Palace, Bradley Orr from Bristol City, Jamie Mackie from Plymouth, Paddy Kenny from Sheffield United and Leon Clarke from Sheffield Wednesday. Added to this was the talismanic Adel Taarabt, although perhaps the most exciting signing had happened the previous season, with the arrival of the experience, guile and leadership of manager Neil Warnock, who really had seen it all, done it all and bought, worn and worn out numerous t-shirts in a long and (sometimes) distinguished career.

The R's had been together for two weeks of intensive training, before heading off to Warnock's future retirement destination in Cornwall. The usual games ensued against eye-catching opposition, such as Bodmin Town and Tavistock AFC, where fans checking for the results could have been forgiven for thinking we had switched allegiance to Rugby Union, such were the six and eight nil scorelines that followed. However, once we played League Two side Torquay, things got a little more real, with the Hoops still running out 3-1 winners.

The players then jetted off to Italy to play two more friendlies (on the premise that 'it allows us to look at different players in different positions and it's all about gaining much needed match fitness'. So why charge us to get in then?) and beat two unheard of sides (I suspect even if you live in Italy) by 4-1 and 2-1, before completing our pre-season matches with a prestige friendly at Loftus Road against... Plymouth Argyle. How the crowds flocked for this one (me not being one of them), as Rangers turned it on to scrape a 1-1 draw, courtesy of a late Jamie Mackie equaliser against the side from which we had signed him.

THE 2010-2011 SEASON IN FULL

The 2010-2011 season in the NPower Championship. Twenty-four teams, all starting out as equals, all with hopes of glory at the end of ten gruelling months that would see forty-six games, home and away, for each side. Once pre-season is over, the serious stuff begins, with two automatic places up for grabs and four playoff places that would decide the third team promoted. The aim: to get back to the 'promised land' of the Premiership, with its wealth of money, not to mention its wealth of talent. QPR had been out of the top flight for some sixteen years, and there was a great deal of hope, as well as a certain element of expectation, that this season could see an end to that wilderness. R's fans craved it just as much as any other side that had seen the Promised Land. However, since our promotion to the then newly named Championship in 2004, Rangers hadn't troubled the top placings or threatened a return to football's elite. So why now? Were we any better equipped to cope with a sustained promotion push this time around?

Barnsley (H)

And so, perhaps with trepidation replacing the injured hope and with optimism on the bench, we kicked off our NPower Championship season with a home game against early alphabetical table toppers Barnsley. Over the years, a fairly tight crowd of us would go on our annual pilgrimage to places 'Up North' and beginning inexplicably with the letter 'B', so we went to Barnsley, Bolton (old and new), Blackpool and Burnley, all of them offering that 'warm' welcome reserved especially for anyone from the South – I could imagine feeling warmer in the North Pole, stark-naked. At Barnsley, for example, we made our way into a local pub, completely deserted apart from two local diehards playing pool. We ordered some ales and hadn't even blown the head off them when a door operative sauntered over.

"Make that your last pint lads," he said. I seem to recall that they were the most quickly consumed pints the world has ever seen, never mind Barnsley.

We chanced asking the restless natives where away fans could get a pint without fear of losing their looks, and were told in grunts of one syllable to try a significantly larger establishment just across the way. I somehow found myself leading the troop, pushing my way through the knee deep red army encapsulating the bar. One glance from the head barman and, even though there was more yelling than in a brothel's happy hour, I could still make out, quite clearly, that "away fans ain't welcome in here". An about turn and we trotted out, single file, to see if we could meet another set of the local jokers to lead us to potential doom.

The next recommended boozer was down a steep hill and, if I didn't know better, looked the perfect location to ambush a group of Cockneys and show them just how hard Northerners are when on home soil, knowing the lay of the local land as they do, and being pre-filled with strong northern tap water. Surprisingly, the pub we found was not only very small, but actually very welcoming, so after lining our stomachs with some of the finest local brew, we made our way back up the hill again and along to Oakwell to witness a fine display of attacking football, slick passing, aggressive tackling and that all important will to win. OK, the team doing this were playing in red, but we did somehow take the lead, which we held until the 94th minute, when incredibly a ball was recycled from the main stand (something that hadn't happened during the rest of the game, as the balls seemed frozen in the Barnsley wind). A superquick throw-in followed, and before we knew it, a trip in the box, a penalty and 'GOOOOAAAALLLL' to the homeside. We made our way back the four-odd hours home, intoxicated and feeling more cheated than a punter in an Amsterdam peepshow.

So, as Joe and I made our way down South Africa Road for the start of another season, the buzz of expectation was evident in the crowd. The programme sellers, who always look like they really want to be somewhere else anyway, touted their publication in the most disinterested way imaginable. The fanzine sellers were back with a far more believable and scathing slant on where they thought the club should be heading, while the badge and scarf vendors (everything unofficial, but always that much more interesting than what's available in the official club shop) were again parading their wares. As for food, the previously mentioned *South Africa Road Fish Bar* still sat proudly in pole position in the parade of shops, still selling the same grub (well, not quite the same as I reckon that would have been off by now), while burger vans (one competitively located outside the fish bar, the other just outside the ground) served the hungry public.

The air was filled with that quintessentially British football ambience, a mixture of cigarette smoke, burgers, beer, horse manure and expectation. Joe and I waited outside the main box office as usual, to meet Queenie and to hopefully top up our growing autograph collection. By chance, we were there as Neil Warnock skipped up to the player's entrance and I ushered Joe forwards to obtain the signature of the man who we all hoped would be the Messiah and take us back to that Promised Land of the Premier League. Joe got his chance and as Neil started the signature, the book and the pen slipped, messing up the page.

"Ooh, sorry son, do you want another one?"

I mention this, as this moment is actually caught on camera for prosperity in Mat Hodgson's fly on the wall documentary *The Four Year Plan*, available from the club shop, just £9.99. And no they didn't pay me to say that. Dammit.

Neil Warnock signing us up (if only!)

The streets were filled with young and old alike, and it's always fascinating to see that mixture of replica shirts from across the years – the classic *Guinness* top of the mid-eighties (still considered by many shirt connoisseurs to be 'the' shirt that defines the R's through the ages), and the black and red 'Dennis The Menace' away shirt its counterpart. This cornucopia of replica shirts of all shapes and sizes ambling down the street I always find compelling, as for many years I too have bought each and every one as they came out and in truth, I collect them. Sad I know, but I have every shirt since about 1990: home and away; third edition (even though we only played in it once all season and even then the second would have sufficed), special 'centenary' edition and finally the once and once only 'limited edition only 300 made' Play Off Final 2003. Plus now I have my son Joe and daughter Katie: Joe has at least two each from the last three seasons, the latest with 'JOE 9' on the back, and the Championship badges (a bargain at £5 a shot), while Katie's first ever shirt was in black and red (as she liked the colours better) with, not surprisingly, 'KATIE 6' on the back. Not to be outdone, I have '40' on the back of mine (yea, it's obvious why) and yes, I succumbed to the badges too. Sadly '40' was the last time I could actually fit into a replica top.

Only there is one big difference between mine and the kids' shirts: they actually wear theirs. Oh, don't get me wrong, I would love to wear mine, especially as it took three hundred and seventeen calls to *QPR Direct* to ascertain when/if I would ever be receiving it and three long hard months for the pre-ordered piece of cloth to actually find its way to the distant isolated flatlands of Norfolk, where I am exiled in purgatory. Having to look at those smug Canaries in their putrid yellow from around July, all decked out in the new strip – OK, they are still crap, but at least theirs were out in time for the season and at least they fit (well in most cases anyway).

And herein lies the problem. I am these days, by my own admission, not the sveltest of personages to grace these windy planes; I do carry the odd stone more than is advised by the NHS. But I am not alone. And if you were stereotyping a father, son and daughter who attend our great game on a Saturday afternoon at 3pm then you may think: forty-something, balding, few stones overweight, likes a pie and a pint at half time, accompanied by a ten and six year old with their names on their shirts and who just love being with their dad. If you have just that picture in your mind's eye, that's me and my kids.

Only something has been different these past few seasons. I have this replica shirt see, but is doesn't bloody fit me! Oh, don't get me wrong, the label says it's an XXXL, which in any other gent's outfitter across the globe would mean you could erect it on your next summer camping trip and comfortably cover a family of four. But when it is designed in Italy, for XXXL read XXXS. I've tried wearing it, but as it's skin tight I look like a pregnant bearded lady. Funny that, as my previous season's shirts fit quite nicely. Yes, the gut is still there, the man boobs are still on show, but I don't feel quite so self-conscious. Oh, how I envy you 'normal' stick insects and your ability to get the size that fits you. My XXXL would probably fit a seventeen year old who hasn't yet taken to the delights of ale and takeaways on a more regular basis, but beware! A few too many in the *Smuts* and the *Wok-A-Holic* over the coming years and you too are also doomed, my friend, to a life wearing replica shirts from days of yore, not because you like *CSF* emblazoned on your chest any more than I do, but because it's the only one that still fits!

Not to worry - the new season is now in full swing, and the three new kits will soon be available to a shirt-starved fan base, so surely we will see the club right itself of the wrongdoings of recent seasons and make shirts that fit the more cuddly of us? Er, no. By all accounts, unless you weigh less than 10 stones and are deprived of height (i.e. under 5' 8) there will be nothing for the likes of you and me to get excited about.

But then it doesn't matter, does it? That's £39.95 of my hard-earned cash the club's not going to get and it's only a piece of cloth when all said and done. Why am I so upset about it? It has no significance in the wider picture. Or do you feel like me? That the shirt is far more important than that? It's our identity, it's what makes us stand out from the others, it's the badge, the colours, it's the Hoops, it's Queens Park Rangers Football Club. I'm sure the deal with *Lotto* is very lucrative, the sponsorship with *Gulf Air* one of the most impressive in club history. I would just love the chance to pull on my shirt during the season, with hope in my heart and cloth on my chest. Sadly, it would appear, that thirty years of continued support for the club I have loved since I was a boy is not enough, and even something that I have taken for granted for so long – wearing the colours – is now reserved for those much smaller and fitter than me. To paraphrase the song historically sung to those players not seen to be giving their all, or who sadly lacked the ability we felt one who plays for the R's should have, 'I am not fit to wear the Hoops'.

Meanwhile, back in the ground, Joe and I took our seats, with Joe already looking forward to Maccy D's on the way home. Rangers gave debuts to Kenny, Mackie, Derry, Hill and

Orr: the team gelled surprisingly quickly and ran out comfortable 4-0 winners. The result of this game remarkably sent us top of the league and Barnsley, in the biggest reverse ever seen, from top to absolute bottom in 90 minutes. Oh how they wished they had been 'Yarnsley', as at least they would have simply remained where they started the day. So, home happy and for one game at least, we were top of the pile. Had someone offered me a four goals without reply and top of the table birth after one match, I would have put it up there with someone also offering me 'Miracle Hair Grow for Men'. But, while any goal is a good one, and here we had feasted on four of the little beauties, none came even close to THAT goal, back in the cup match in 1997 at Loftus Road, against today's opponents Barnsley and scored by Rangers legend 'Clever' Trevor Sinclair – a match which I was lucky enough to attend.

I remember it well (not as I have some sort of photographic memory, but because it actually won the *BBC's Goal of the season* and I have therefore seen the clip many times over the years). As the ball was swung in from the right (as we looked at it from the other end of the ground in the Upper Loft), Sinclair, with his back to goal, leapt highest and, with incredible ferocity, scissor-kicked the ball right-footed into the back of the Barnsley net. It really was one of those moments where you can say 'I was there', as applause rang around the ground, even from the away section behind the goal. Or maybe they were just celebrating the devouring of a particularly excellent meat pie. Hmm, this is the Rangers stadium, so maybe it was the goal after all, because it really was one of those where even the opposing manager can't say, as they are prone to do, "I'm disappointed with our defending" or "we should have got tighter to the man". It was simply fantastic: an outstanding piece of individual brilliance. Would I take that goal as payment for our appalling record in the competition since that game? Of course. That was a moment, one to tag together with all those other moments that make up our memories and the rich tapestry of our football lives.

Port Vale (H)

Next up and with a welcome (coughs, it's been one game dammit!) break from the pressures of the league campaign, a seemingly easy home *Carling Cup* match against Port Vale. Perhaps predictably (if you look back over Rangers' recent cup exploits) we bowed out at the first hurdle 1-3, to give that well used cliché "it will give us a chance to concentrate on the league" another much unneeded airing.

Unlike this game, one of Rangers' greatest ever comebacks was also against Vale, in a league match back in 1997, which, for some inexplicable reason, was televised. I remember having Mum and Dad round my place, where, to show my independence, I cooked lunch and we all watched the match together. If my culinary (lack of) talents weren't bad enough, Rangers were metaphorically still sitting on the team coach playing cards, as in forty-five of the worst minutes in living memory, we found ourselves 4-0 down! I know how badly I took it, as I went and did the washing up, cursing under my breath and scraping the plates so hard the authentic Willow pattern was peeling off. Had I actually been there, I think I may have been hitching a lift home at half time, rather than wait for the supporters' coach, it really had been that bad.

When the second half got under way, I was still finishing off in the kitchen, muttering to myself, and, being that annoyed, kicking the cat. Strange, as I didn't have a cat at the time, but had gone outside and asked politely to borrow next door's for the very purpose, which they reluctantly agreed to, and by the look I must have given them, figured the cat was a better option than me kicking them, or their Koi Carp. I hadn't missed anything on my return to the living room, and was really just hoping for the whistle, when after sixty-six minutes, Vale took pity and scored for us – better than we'd managed to do for ourselves up to that point. It seemed unlikely they would do it three more times, but I lived in hope – something you learn to do over the years as a Hoop.

With five minutes to go and seemingly little probability of even another consolation, Rangers scored again through Andy Impey. I remember a faint leap and a 'YES!', but no more.

When Paul Murray scored our third, suddenly the most unlikely of comebacks was now on the cards. Had I now been hurtling down the motorway having hitched a ride, I would have been asking them to turn the car around and take us back to Stoke-on-Trent, as a miracle on a par with a picture of Jesus crying real tears was unfolding at Vale Park. As injury time was upon us, Danny Dichio's effort was saved, only for John 'Spenny' Spencer to smash the ball home to make it 4-4! The fact that as he scored he was just feet away from the away supporters must have been an amazing moment for those that went! It was pretty special just watching it on the telly, my celebrations clearly the birth of what was to come years later, with me leaping around the room kicking furniture and shouting "YYYYYYYYYEEEEEEEESSSSSSSSS!!!!" at the top of my voice, forcing elderly neighbours to stay indoors with their pets.

Just a note on John Spencer: for a couple of seasons he was excellent for us in what was, let's be honest, a pretty poor side overall and at a time when the club really were on a downward spiral. Spencer signed for the club at the same time as Gavin Peacock (another excellent acquisition), both coming from Chelscum, but clearly their move was in the best interests of all concerned. I was actually there for their debuts, a 2-1 defeat at Reading's old Elm Park stadium, with Spencer scoring. If memory serves me correctly, so was Queenie, but this is where it often fails me, as to exactly who was at which game.

It's weird, sometimes my memory is crisp and my knowledge almost anal, as I can remember games, results, scorers, etc., whilst others I can't. I can't even put it down to "Oh, it was the sixties and we were all high man": firstly as it was the nineties so that wouldn't wash at all, and secondly the closest I have been to high was on a climbing wall on a team building course in Milton Keynes, and even then 'high' is a misnomer, as I only made it to the first climbing hold before retiring, hurt, giddy and with a small nose bleed, self-inflicted when I pulled out a small clump of nasal hair too fast while nobody was looking, just to get me out of an event that truly terrified me.

Sheff Utd (A)

Fortunately we faired a tad better in our next match - the first away day of the new season - at Sheffield United. I was wandering around the 'fine' shops of Norwich with the family after another average morning at the office, when my phone bleeped to tell me the team 'apple'. For those of you not *au fait* with the London lingo, the 'apple' was something Queenie and I used as an abbreviation from Cockney rhyming slang, the 'apple core' being the 'score'. We used it for pretty much anything, so the opening gambit "Alright, what's the apple?", could mean "What's the score?" or could just mean "What's happening?". Whenever the phone went again fairly soon after, it normally meant a goal, with me praying it was going to say 'xxx opposition 0 QPR 1' and the name of the hero of the day. Lo and behold it did indeed say 'Blades 0 QPR 1 (Ephraim)'.

At this point I hope I hear nothing more until about 5pm and the confirmation that we have won 1-0 (see, I'm not greedy like that), but soon after my phone bleeped again. Being a Rangers fan, and therefore owner of a glass that is half-empty, cracked and worthless, my heart said "please let it be 0-2" but my head was saying "shut up you nutter, of course it's 1-1, we just caught them on the hop and they have now woken up", but was amazed to see we were indeed two goals to the good, and that Jamie Mackie had scored his second goal in two games.

Now at this point a kind of madness descends, where you start working out permutations of how, if it stays like this, we would be top for a second game running, having scored six without reply and probably our best start in 300 years or something. I was briefly awoken from this fantasy by my phone bleeping yet again, and was almost beyond belief when I saw Queenie's text showing 0-3 (Taarabt pen), so much so that I nearly fell over on the cobbled streets of Elm Hill. Thankfully my phone bleeped no more. We had won and had now scored seven goals without reply – top for a second week!

Ah, but we weren't, as amazingly Millwall also had two wins from two games, scoring seven and conceding none, so led the table - you guessed it - alphabetically! I felt cheated! I mean, Rangers were never top and with what we had notched up so far why couldn't we be top still?!

Scunny (H)

Our next game was against unfancied Scunthorpe, typically a game that Rangers would capitulate historically. For this, I had the usual text alerts from Queenie, but I also listened on *QPR Player*: the live commentary service provided by the club. As a concept it's great, giving folk like me, exiled in Norwich, the chance to hear the matches we can't attend. The problem is when the connection drops out at their end and you are left looking at nothing, hearing nothing and frantically trying to reconnect. Don't get me wrong, for many years this would have been a godsend, not being able to hear another atrocity unfolding, particularly away from home. But when you are alphabetically second and success-starved, you crave every minute of every game, as you know it may well not last.

Unpredictably we won again, this time 2-0, and with Millwall only drawing, we found ourselves a clear first, nine points from nine, nine goals scored, none conceded and leading the rest of the pack. I was half expecting to wake up at some point and find that it was actually three straight defeats, nine goals conceded and none scored, but no matter where I looked, in the papers, on the official and unofficial sites and the BBC league tables, it was the same! We were actually top!

One comedy classic that was recorded for prosperity was something called the *Fanzone*, where a supporter from each club goes in a booth and basically rambles on for the entire match. Both fans are dressed in the replica shirt (just in case you can't work out who supports who), and basically it's a free-for-all with mikes up close, and the chance to go head-to-head with your opposite equivalent. For this match, the Scunny guy was brilliant, as we watch his demise on camera, while the Rangers guy clearly loves it, just like us! It's ninety minutes of in-your-face banter, so quite how the losing supporter doesn't deck the other is amazing!

Derby (A)

As we were now important, news was that our next match, away to Derby County, was to be streamed live, a very exciting prospect, as I'd be able to see for myself how the team were faring and whether we could continue our rampant start to the campaign. I sat in my home office (aka the converted cupboard adjoining our 'family room') and feverishly searched various sites (some of questionable legality) for a stream to follow. About ten minutes in (and with much swearing and questioning of the parentage of the websites owners) I found myself live at Pride Park and watching the game. Now, I have always been very honest about my team, trying not to watch through the blue and white rimmed spectacles (adjust colour of said spectacles to that of your own team's colours to obtain same effect) that some fans seem to see their beloved team through. So on this occasion it was fair to say, in my humble opinion, we were crap.

Derby took a deserved lead just before half time and I thought "Oh well. At least we can't play any worse in the second half", but we did, and Derby scored again. The game was effectively over, and so was our record. This was more like the away day shambles we had grown to know and loathe, more 'Queens Park Strangers' than Queens Park Rangers. With time almost up, I rang Queenie, who I knew hadn't gone to the game, to give him an update.

"How can I delight you?" was his normal salutation.

"Just giving you an apple. You watching or listening?"

"Nah, after hearing us go 2-0 down I turned off *Player*."

"Well, it's still 2-0 Barbie (my derogatory name for them) and we have played pony (Cockney rhyming slang – pony and trap = crap). Don't deserve to get anything today, second best all over the park."

The game carried on in the background as I continued my analysis:

"We've been found out today. Maybe it's bringing in too many new players... hang on, Agyemang has burst through, go on Pat, take him on, he's got his shot off and IT'S IN! HANG ON, WE'RE BACK IN IT!!!!

"Too little, too late though. Hold it, there are five additional minutes! You may as well stay with me live!" Four minutes into stoppage time and Derby break away.

"That's it, they're gonna finish us off now, 3-1! NO! Great save Paddy Kenny! Now launch it! Last chance saloon! He's gone long. Good flick on by Agyemang to Mackie edge of the box. Go on son, hit it, take him on, hit it, he's through; shoot, bottom corner…

"YYYYYYYYEEEEEEEESSSSSSSSS!!!! MACKIE FOR RANGERS! GET IN THERE!!!! GET IN!!!! RANGERS ARE LEVEL! OMG, HOW THE F*** HAVE WE GOT A POINT OUT OF THIS!!!! THE FANS HAVE GONE CHICKEN (oriental = mental) BEHIND THE GOAL!!!! THEY'RE OFF THE BENCH!!!! FULL SHIRT OFF, FULL TATTOOS, FULL PHYSIQUE!!!!"

I was literally screaming down the phone and convinced I had caused Queenie irreversible hearing damage, as I kicked my wheelie chair and punched the door with delight, possibly breaking a small bone in my hand in the process. I flicked on the TV, still punching the air and shouting "YES!" through gritted teeth, tuning in to see that we still led the league, albeit only on goal difference now, from Cardiff (affectionately called Baadiff) and Ipswich (or Ipsh*t), as Queenie and I continued our after-match warm down, signing off with the usual "Ta-da".

Middlesbrough (H)

Next up at Loftus Road were Middlesbrough, another team languishing in the lower reaches of the league, keen to take on the leaders in their own back yard and knock them off their lofty perch. Although having said that, I'm not sure if one would be on a perch in their own back yard. Front room maybe. But anyway. I settled in for another afternoon in front of the *iMac* and the frustration that is *QPR Player*. After a pulsating (not) goalfest first 45 (so in other words 0-0), Rangers came out and blitzed their lowly counterparts with three second half goals, from Helguson, Ephraim and that man Jamie Mackie again. Not surprisingly, we still led the field, still only on goal difference though, as Baadiff had won again. Ipswich were two points behind in third, and it was they who we played next, at Portman Road, home of the Tractor Boys.

Ipswich (A)

As Ipswich is the proverbial stone's throw from us (albeit you would have to have some forearm to launch a stone nearly fifty miles, but in football away day terms it's a manageable one) and an annual fave for me and Joe, not to mention that we were able to obtain tickets, we set off, with hope in our hearts and a firm belief that we could continue our unbeaten start to the season.

I have been going to Ipswich for many years, mainly due to its relative closeness, not for the scenery or splendid array of shopping facilities. It's been a mixed venue emotionally, rather like their friends down the road in Norwich, where I have seen the usual away day misery (2-0 comes to mind on a few too many occasions, although we have won with the same scoreline, Dan Shittu scoring the second at the far end of the ground, much to my and Queenie's delight) but also a famous 4-1 win, with crowd favourite, Rob Steiner, scoring at least once that day. Queenie and I reached the conclusion we had jinxed the team that year, by getting numbers on the backs of our replica shirts for the first time, not because we were sad or anything, but that the shirts had this huge white space on the back that called out to be filled with a digit, like a prostate doctor needs to fill something else with a digit of a slightly different variety. The players whose numbers we had chosen to have on the home and away shirts both went on to sustain cruciate ligament injuries that effectively ruined them for not only this season, but as is so often the case, for the remainder of their careers, with players just never returning the same again.

This season's Ipswich match was an evening affair, and as was usual, we were to meet Queenie around the station, as he too was attending, and by train. We arrived on time (and at the time we said we would), but surprise surprise! Queenie was nowhere to be seen, and on calling him, we discovered he was still some twenty minutes away. Queenie's time keeping (or lack of it) was legendary. I would be travelling 100 miles and could always be within a few minutes of arriving when I said I would, while Queenie would be coming a fraction of the distance, but was rarely on time, usually as a result of not getting to bed until 4am due to a mini-cabbing job. Joe and I would often find ourselves standing at London Liverpool Street station awaiting our promised lift, and even though we had been in constant contact via mobiles, Queenie could be guaranteed to hit a pocket of traffic somewhere that would delay him. I did suggest (often) that if he left his house earlier, he could legislate for any traffic he may come across. He did retort (often) that I should shut my mouth or get a tube. In other words, the same old banter.

As we were kicking about doing nothing, Joe and I made our way to the local Maccy D for tea and awaited contact from Major Tom. There was still time to go and pick up a programme from outside the ground, so we made our way back up the hill to the station, but there was still no sign. The next thing Queenie called to say he was outside the ground and wanted to know where we were! So back we went and eventually caught up with him. As usual, he set about play-fighting with Joe and the usual slates between us were in plentiful supply. Once inside, he ordered his customary glut of hot dogs, claiming he was starving and hadn't had time to eat.

I started to get nervous, as with our previous mixed track record here, it really was a case of which Rangers would turn up. Also making his debut for the R's was Kyle Walker, a much talked about and fancied right back, on loan from Spurs. As the game got underway, Joe was a bit restless, but soon calmed down as Jamie Mackie pounced on a half chance and put the R's ahead 1-0! I went absolutely berserk and the crowd, always in good voice, started singing Mackie's new song (to the tune of *Winter Wonderland*) "There's only one Jamie Mackie, one Jamie Mackie, walking along, singing a song, walking in a Mackie Wonderland!".

Things went from good to even better, as a sweeping move saw Mackie burst through the centre and he ran and ran and ran (with Walker making a dash down the right side and stretching the Town defence in the process), before drilling a low shot into the bottom corner. 2-0 and the travelling hoards went mental (me included) as we just couldn't believe what we were seeing! The songs began to flow: "Taarabt, Taarabt, Taarabt, Taarabt, Taarabt, Taarabt, Taarabt, Adel Taarabt" (to the tune of the *Pink Panther*) and "We're top of the league, we're top of the league, we're Queens Park Rangers, we're top of the league", plus "About f***ing time, about f***ing time, Rangers are back, about f***ing time".

By the time Helguson slotted away the penalty midway through the second half, having actually scored what appeared to be a perfectly good goal just seconds before through Akos Buzsaky, with what I recall was one of the hardest strikes I have ever seen, the game was up, with some Ipswich fans having seen enough and exiting the ground very early. Rangers fans were loving every second, and I felt a warmth through the cold night air that I hadn't felt in many a long year. A real feeling that we had the players, the manager and the BELIEF that this really could be the start of something very special. As fans around me started to do the conga up and down the aisles, this really had been a great night. What could be better than watching your team, top of the league, playing away from home, scoring another three goals without reply, with your son and your best football mate? OK a lottery win, a *Jacuzzi* bath in Hugh Heffner's mansion while he was away on business and a simple, free and painless operation for hair regrowth may be up there, but for me, nights like this were ahead of the game.

As the final whistle went, the Rangers players came over to applaud our support and I said to Joe "Clap the players mate. You won't get many nights like this as a rule, enjoy them while they last."

As we made our way out of the ground, and with our train some time away, we said our goodbyes to Queenie and made our way back to Maccy D's for a hot chocolate, before heading home, tired, but immensely happy and proud. It was a lovely moment, as if Joe had suddenly grown up and I was going to a match with a mate, while for him, I sensed (as is common) that he just liked spending time with his dad, like I had done all those years ago with my father, Maccy D's thermal cups the modern equivalent to our old thermos flask, the hot chocolate replacing the tomato soup that Mum used to pack us off with.

Leicester (A)

Rangers' next test of the unbeaten record was to come at Leicester, a dangerous encounter, as they were the wrong end of the table, and with expectations high (along with the amount of money being spent), it may only be a matter of time before they got their season off and running. I just hoped it wasn't going to be today and my wish was to come true! An early goal from the in-form Jamie Mackie, looping his header out of the reach of former R's loanee Karl Ikeme, set us on our way, and even though we were under the cosh for much of the second half, it was that man Mackie again, jinking into the Leicester box and slotting away coolly, that secured the three points and sent the travelling fans into raptures.

One thing that had become prevalent this season was people putting up *YouTube* clips of our celebrations, seen from a fans-eye view. The ones from our previous away day at Ipswich helped capture some of the great atmosphere that night, and indeed I have seen myself, Queenie and Joe, albeit really quickly, going mad in the masses! The second Mackie goal at Leicester has been beautifully captured for prosperity, in that the build-up is shown as well, and you sense how, as a fan, you start to see passes that you want players to make (easy from way up high in the stands, of course), and watch an attack unfolding, then start to edge forward on your seat as you spot the possibility of a killer pass, or a movement that may end in a strike, or better still a goal. The way the scene of Mackie's second goal pans out goes from the team playing the ball about in non-dangerous areas, and the crowd simply following the play, to Mackie pouncing on the opportunity on the edge of the area and the crowd suddenly becoming alive to the possibility of an end product, to the audible gasp of expectation and cries of "Go on!" and "Take him ON!", before that sound that proceeds a goal being scored, where everyone seems to suck in all the air in the ground, releasing it in the elation of seeing the net bulge and the ecstasy that we had all but won again.

So we now had an incredible nineteen points from a maximum possible twenty-one, and murmurs of "best ever start to the season" and "promotion already in the bag" (from some quarters) began.

Donny Rovers (H)

It was back to HQ for the visit of Doncaster Rovers, having made a good start to the season and only just outside the playoff positions themselves. This was another 'Queenie World Service' text update, in collaboration with *QPR Player* afternoon – never ideal, but still a far cry from the bad old days of having only the *BBC World Service* who might give the score of the Rangers game (if you were lucky), so you listened intently to the entire show, just in case and to make sure you didn't miss it. I can honestly say I don't remember much about this match, with a goalless first forty-five, but a rip-rousing second seeing us score yet another three goals, thereby cementing our position at the top of the table, and indeed extending our lead to six points over our nearest rivals Baadiff.

It's during games like these that even I can become partly distracted, instead choosing to spend a few minutes checking our *Daily Mail Fantasy League* progress. Our team...

'Downafiverforregisteringateamthatwillneverwini namillionyears'

...is already in danger of expulsion from the league for betting irregularities. I'm not sure if being 48,342nd in the country is really that great, or the fact that since joining, I now seem to get invited on a daily basis to hook up with lonely Indonesian lap dancers on my email account. Do they think I am that stupid, desperate or lonely to actually respond? Well, not for a second time anyway...

144

Millwall (H)

With a six point cushion, this stood us in good stead for our first London derby of the season, with Millwall next up at Loftus Road. I had to endure a bit of a build-up to this one, as a work colleague supported the Lions, so there was a bit of banter along the lines of them taking our unbeaten record. I took this in good humour, and made him a coffee with cold water, shredded his sandwiches, and hid his favourite expensive pen.

The game proved to be a stalemate and a lively match ended with no goals to show for either side's endeavours. Again, I had sat listening to every kick, with the usual 'oohs' and 'aahhs' as Rangers came close on more than one occasion, balanced with the 'phews' and 's**t' as the commentator tried to tell us just how close the opposition had come. Still, a point kept us six clear at the summit, with a mightily impressive goal difference of plus twenty, also securing our eighth clean sheet of the campaign, and bringing a highly successful September to a close.

Palarse (A)

October started with another London derby, this time with a trip to South East London to play Crystal Palace, who in stark contrast to ourselves, were languishing at the wrong end of the table in the relegation zone. This match had obviously captured the imagination of some Iraqi channel, and was available for live streaming. Whilst my Arabic isn't terribly efficient, my eyes can still make out a Hoop from an Eagle, so with sound down, I tucked into what I hoped would be another away day feast.

Now, the more technically minded might just be wondering why I didn't simply run the audio commentary on *QPR Player* with the visuals from *Al Jazeera*. Well, yours truly has done this in the past; however, the two are not simultaneous, and I have actually heard a goal scored where the picture would indicate otherwise! It's the strangest concept, as your head can't get around that somebody, somewhere seems to be lying!

Still, in anyone's language, the match was all square at half time, with neither side able to trouble the scorers.

The second half burst into life after just four minutes, with Palace's Edgar Davids (yes, he of the oversized glasses and distinguished career of playing for Holland and for top sides in Europe, yes THAT Edgar Davids, now playing for a relegation threatened Crystal Palace) playing a suicide ball back to his keeper and not legislating for the customary wet Selhurst Park pitch holding the ball up sufficiently for that man Mackie to burst clear, round the keeper, do a little jig, have a quick shower, perform a two minute audition for *The X Factor* and tee the ball up for the 'mercurial Moroccan' Adel Taarabt to slot home. Evidently Mackie and 'Tarbs' had a small falling out during the half time oranges, I believe over the fact that Mackie is a wholehearted team player and Adel is known as 'two balls', not due to any kind of smutty innuendo, but that he needs one ball just for himself while the team play with the other. Whatever was said (second guess would be)...

> Mackie to Adel: Pass the ball you greedy b***ard.
> Adel to Mackie: Get your own, you mouthy t**t.

...had certainly done the trick, because I was screaming at the screen myself.

"Take him on Mackie, he's round the keeper, cross it to the unmarked Taarabt... YYYYEEEESSSSSSSS!!!! GET IN!!!!"

My American friend Freddy, who was actually round that afternoon, was in the kitchen preparing our tea (he loves to do such things, so don't feel too sorry for him, and he's a great cook, while my house speciality is *Frosties* with milk) and shouted out "Did they score or something?"

Greatly understated on occasion, these Americans. As the match wore on, I became increasingly agitated for the final whistle, as a single goal lead is never really enough at any level. With just a minute to go, the unthinkable happened, and Palace equalised. By my reaction and the splintering of my wooden computer desk, Freddy could tell I wasn't overly happy.

"1-1," I huffed. "It's been coming though."

And suddenly those doubts you have as a football fan start to rise to the surface, having gone from "just a few more minutes and we have three more points", to "can we hold on for one, and is that such a bad result?". But as injury time was being played out, Tommy Smith swung in a hopeful cross to the back stick, and there was Heidar Helguson, rising like the proverbial salmon, to get head and shoulders above Palace keeper Julian Speroni and guide his header into the back of the net. It was one of those moments where your initial thoughts are:

1. He has bundled into the keeper;
2. The keeper is protesting, the ref always goes to protect the keeper, so the goal won't stand;
3. He was offside;
4. The linesman's not given it.

All this packed into about two seconds in reality, and time seems to stand still. I was up out of my wheelie chair, desperately trying to determine and decipher inaudible Arabic and failing quite obviously, and almost craning my neck round to see what the linesman was saying, when out of my mouth came the loudest "YYYYYYYYEEEEEEEESSSSSSSS!!!!" to date!

We had snatched it! We had won again!!!! Having now played ten games and only dropped four points – it was the stuff of dreams! Freddy came in to see what all the commotion was about, having nearly dropped his fresh pasta sauce creation, such was my screaming and inexplicable kicking of my wheelie chair (which I actually like and it has never done anything to me) and punching of the family room door (that's never done anything to me either).

"Did QPR score?" he enquired.

"They sure did!!!!" I said, with an American twang to my voice that just kind of seemed right at that moment. As the pictures disappeared I flicked the TV on to see *Sky Sports*

News, to check how the table now stood after today's results, so I could visualise us still sitting at the top for another week.

I called Queenie for his take and our customary after-match synopsis. Understandably he was happy with the day's events, not so the journey there and back, which we had both done on numerous occasions and almost seemed to take as long as getting to Blackburn. There was also always a notable lack of atmosphere at Selhurst Park. That said, all fans think their lot out-sing the home fans, while home fans always say that the away fans never turn up in great quantities, with chants of "is that all you take away?" being met with "is that all you have at home?"

Queenie had to call off as he wanted to start his train journey back, and knew that on a good day he wouldn't arrive home until at least next Saturday – perhaps an over-exaggeration, but it's not a pleasant journey, OK?!

Norwich (H)

16.10.10: QPR v Norwich City at Loftus Road.

The 'big one' had arrived, and myself, Joe and a friend Alex (a Canary) from work set off by train, destination: London Liverpool Street, en route to the Mecca. As you would expect, there was loads of banter between us, with Joe giving Alex a masterclass in *Uno* cards, reading the daily rags and eating various parts of our packed lunch. I was especially nervous that day, as Norwich were going great guns and I really didn't want to lose the unbeaten run, to them of all teams.

We met Queenie before the game as usual and Alex was introduced to the 'legend', to exchange slates and talk about their respective teams. Our seats were as part of a giveaway in *The Sun*, so pricewise we were quids in, but on the downside our seats, although still in the home area in Ellerslie Road, were almost within touching distance of the away end, so at least Alex felt at home. I sportingly touched fists with him just before kick-off, and could easily have gone higher and knocked him out – not for any other reason than he was a

Canary. I would have struggled reaching him of course, unless I was prepared to stand on one of our plastic seats, with the name of that season's 'owner' written on a sticky label in biro and classily stuck on the back with *Pritt* stick, but figured my weight would probably see me break the seat in two and leave me sprawled on the deck.

The game got under way and the first notable event was that Norwich were awarded a penalty, Clint Hill adjudged to have blown too hard on City legend Grant Holt, a master of going down under the challenge of a strong breeze. Wes 'Hooligan' Hoolihan stepped up to take it, but bottled it when he saw all those R's fans packed in behind Paddy Kenny's goal, willing him to trip over his laces. He didn't quite manage that, but did the next best thing and dragged his terrible penalty wide, thus achieving cult status in my book forever more (unless he managed to score against us, in which case he will be instantly crossed off my Christmas card list).

Rangers had more of the play second half but at the final whistle, the spoils were shared, and we could all go home miserable. The customary Maccy D was purchased and consumed on the way back, with a few more games of *Uno* and numerous games on the *iPhone* to while away the two hour journey. Positives of the day: another clean sheet, still top of the league and Joe whipping Alex's butt at cards!

One great story to come from the game first started when I watched an interview with Paddy Kenny taken after the match, during which he talks about obtaining the shirt that Wes 'My Hero' Hoolihan had worn during the match itself, and then giving said shirt to a lad of a Canary supporting friend from up in Sheffield who had come down to follow their team. Some days later I was trawling *eBay*, as you do, looking for tat that I could sell on at a small profit, such as my rare copies of All About Eve's first album (fully signed) or *Disney's Greatest Hits* on not so rare black vinyl, when I noticed a rather unique item that was for sale. It was a match worn Wes Hoolihan shirt v QPR! The description was classic, it basically said:

"I obtained the shirt from my friend Paddy Kenny, who had obtained it for me at my request, as my son is a big fan of Wes.

However, since the penalty miss, he now likes Grant Holt!"

On reflection, I should have purchased the shirt and displayed it on my wall. While my Canary neighbours would have thought I had been under the scalpel and had a lobotomy, I could have reminded them that it was 'Sir Wes' that helped us maintain our unbeaten start!

Swansea (A)

Swansea City stood in the way of Rangers equalling their best ever start to a season. With *Player* fired up, Joe and I sat and listened to the game and it wasn't long before we had conceded our second penalty in as many matches. If it's at all humanly possible to will someone to miss a penalty by closing your eyes and clenching your hands tightly together, while listening to a match hundreds of miles away, then I was giving it every chance of working. I was expecting to hear the home crowd cheering the opener, but I was leaping up and down myself when I heard "And Kenny has saved it!".

I must confess that I don't really remember anything else of note, although I think a point and another clean sheet was a fair return from another tough away fixture.

Bristol City (A)

Next up was a *Sky Sports* Friday night live match away at Bristol City. Now, as most fans will tell you, when your match is going out to the nation, you tend to capitulate and show everyone just how lucky you are to be where you are in the league, the glare of the lights almost becoming too much for some, and even the simplest of tasks, like passing the ball to a team mate, becomes impossible. The opposition however seem to raise their game, and this match was no exception, with Jon Stead smashing in a shot from about 75 yards that beat Paddy Kenny all ends up. I would wager my kitten that if he hit that same shot another 50 times, those standing behind the goal would have more chance of being killed by his *Exocet* missile of a strike than him ever seeing it hit the back of the net again.

The goal understandably put Rangers on the back foot, and

for the rest of the game we huffed and puffed, but still we couldn't blow the City house down. Or at least, not until the 82nd minute, when big Pat Agyemang finally restored parity and ensured that the club made history by making it officially Rangers' best ever start to a league campaign. The win kept us top, but now only three clear of Baadiff, who still had a game in hand.

Burnley (H)

Rangers' next game was against a bit of a bogey side in Burnley. Our recent record against the Clarets was nothing short of grim, but this season's side were made of sterner stuff. Could we secure a win back at fortress Loftus Road? Short answer: no, but we remained unbeaten, Adel Taarabt's great strike not done justice by *Player*, then cancelled out by yet another penalty conceded, this time duly dispatched by Graham Alexander, unofficially the world's oldest player at 87. The bad news about this fourth consecutive draw was that we relinquished the top spot to Baadiff for the first time (properly) this season (if you discount the earlier farce of being knocked off top spot by nature of the alphabet).

Reading (H)

With four draws out of five matches in October, it was important to try and return to our winning ways at the start of November, and first up to hopefully oblige us with three points was Reading, or the 'Fake Hoops' as they have been donned by irate R's fans desperate to remind the footballing world that we are the real deal when it comes to the blue and white hooped home shirt. This was another game where *QPR Player* stood in to provide me with a link to the Rangers Stadium, nicely complimenting Queenie's normal team news (including subs) and post-match summary.

Rangers took the lead from the spot, the increasingly impressive Taarabt opening the scoring, but then Bradley Orr, back in the side after Walker had looked to have made the right back berth his own, let the occasion get the better of him and was duly sent off for trying to decapitate the brilliantly named Hal Robson Kanu, presumably for having a longer name than him, which clearly is nearly always going to be the case when your surname is only three letters in total.

Undeterred, Rangers extended their lead in the second half through midfield magician Ali Faurlin. When Reading pulled one back with about twenty minutes to go, my nerves were jangling louder than a chav's necklace on a winter's night, but I need not have worried, as Tommy Smith scored his first goal for the club to see us home and hosed (a saying I still don't understand, as I have never seen anyone arrive home and get washed down by the fire service). The win was important, as it stopped the drawing sequence and also lifted us back to top spot.

Pompey (A)

Fratton Park, home of Pompey Portsmouth, was the next stop on the Rangers rollercoaster, where we were now unbeaten in 15 league matches. Rangers donned their poppy shirts for this one, and there was certainly a fair bit of charity floating about when Matt Connolly was adjudged to have brought down Dave Kitson in the box and a penalty was duly awarded. It was never a penalty ref, anyone can see that, even me, sitting here in my office listening on *QPR Player*!

A quick aside about referees (no book is complete without a word or three hundred for the 'Men in Black'). What a tough job they have, as well as the linesmen, or lineswomen sometimes of course, or third officials as they are now to be called. I say tough, it must be, when they watch players running around earning fifty-five pounds a MINUTE (yea, I am sad and did work it out, but you have to know that as a writer I have to do the research, just like if I was auditioning for a part in the remake of *Crossroads* I would take along my very own 'Benny' hat and have practiced a West Country accent for days beforehand). Perhaps it's the disparity between their earnings and those of the superstar players that makes them sometimes come across as bitter and twisted, the sense of power the only thing they have (well, that and red and yellow cards, a notebook, pen and whistle). Many must be failed actors, as they always seem to want to be centre stage. How many games have you attended where their whistle-happy antics have made your blood boil? Where from your vantage point you only have eyes for your own team? When you are away and those vital decisions go against you, you naturally call them 'homers' (along with the inevitable questioning of their parentage or their solo nocturnal leanings involving adult reading material in pictures, baby oil and a box of man-sized tissues)?

Meanwhile, back at the match, Connolly also saw red for his trouble and it really did start to feel like the run was going to come to an end. But then hope sprang eternal and Kenny saved Liam Lawrence's spot kick! YES!!!! But then he had to retake it and he scored. NO!!!!

As time ticked on I began to fear the worst. Well, it had to happen sooner or later, I thought, somewhat philosophically, while still keeping a shred of hope that we could somehow turn it around one more time. Then, just as I was putting the finishing touches to my hangman's noose, Liam Lawrence handled in the box and the R's were given a lifeline to salvage a point. Lawrence must have broken a mirror after scoring his twice taken penalty, as his luck more than ran out - not only did he concede the penalty, but also collected his second yellow card for his continued protestations.

"It's just not FAIR," he wasn't overheard saying.

As he trudged off he would have noticed further irony, as up stepped Tommy Smith, still officially on the books at Pompey after a bodged deadline day transfer by Rangers meant we could only take the player on loan until January, striding up confidently to tuck away a last gasp equaliser that Sir Alex would have been proud of.

"YYYYYYYYYEEEEEEEESSSSSSSSS!!!!   GET   IN!!!! HAVE SOME OF THAT POMPEY!!!!"

Another draw and we clung on for another game undefeated.

Forest (A)

Another tough away game followed a few days later, as the boys headed to the Midlands to entertain Nottingham Forest, with former R's favourites Lee Camp and Dexter Blackstock turning out for the home side. I'm sure I listened to this, but have no recollection of the game whatsoever, the scoreline of 0-0 may bear testament to that fact, or I may just have had one too many a small Irish that evening. It did however take us to seventeen matches undefeated, with another clean sheet, although we dropped back down to second again in the overall league standings, one point behind our friends from Baadiff and in a bizarre Welsh sandwich, six points ahead of Swansea City, who themselves were finding their form. The greatest thing about not conceding a goal to Forest, or certainly not going 1-0 down at least, is their inability to chant the following at us:

"1-0, 1-0, 1-0, 1-0" (but pronounced 'wan-nil, wan-nil, wan-nil, wan-nil in a very false 'mockney' accent).

Over the years I have witnessed some great chanting between home and away supporters, largely good-natured and often hugely creative. To hear your own supporters giving the opposition 'verbals' is quite satisfying in itself, and can often dampen the tension in a game. Below I have listed some of my favourites:

- "If you can't talk proper shut ya mouth, if you can't talk proper shut ya mouth, if you can't talk proper, can't talk proper, can't talk proper shut ya mouth" (to the tune of *She'll be coming round the mountain when she comes.*)

- "Chim chiminee, chim chiminee, chim chim cheroo, who needs Sol Campbell when we've got Shittu?"

- "Your s***, and you stink of fish!" (Rangers fans to Grimsby fans, all thirty-seven of them. They don't travel well. A bit like their fish.)

- "About f***ing time, about f***ing time, Rangers are back, about f***ing time!" (heard at various times throughout the

2010-2011 season, but my recollection was at Ipswich.)

- "Taarabt, Taarabt, Taarabt, Taarabt, Taarabt, Taarabt, Taarabt, Adel Taarabt." (to the theme tune of the *Pink Panther.)*

- "Up ya arse, and up ya arse, you stick the blue flag up ya arse, from Stamford Bridge to Wembley, you stick the blue flag up ya arse!!!!"

- "Six foot two, eyes of blue, Stevie Wicks is after you, la la la la la la la la la."

- "We'll be there, when Glen, goes up, to lift the FA Cup. We'll be there, we'll be there." (to captain Glen Roeder in 1982. Sadly I wasn't and sadly he didn't.)

- "You're fat, and your bird's a s**g!" (to a Southampton fan at the old 'Dell' who was giving the travelling fans verbals, only for his girlfriend to follow suit and dance somewhat more provocatively than her fella would normally allow her to do in public, to a stand packed with somewhat inebriated away fans, much to his horror.)

- "We're the finest football team, the world has ever seen."

Now I may be a mad keen Hoop (if you hadn't guessed already) but really? The finest? The world has EVER seen? Call me old fashioned, but have you watched Barcelona, or Real Madrid this season maybe? Man United in their prime perhaps? Liverpool of the eighties or Nottingham Forest of the late seventies? Or Brazil down the years. I will defend my boys to the hilt, as would any discerning fan, but I have to disagree here. I have seen Tony Scully, Keith Rowland and Chris Kiwomya in the same team and if you had too, you may well be tempted to change some of the words, such as 'finest' to 'crappiest'.

PNE (H)

Back to Loftus Road for the visit of the rock bottom side Preston North End. Surely we wouldn't capitulate to the bottom side? Oh yes, we have been here before with Rangers, many times, with expectations high that we would turn up, score a bucketful, and all go home happy. Adel is that good he could take them all on, singlehandedly, hands (and feet) tied behind his back!

Rangers started brightly and Rob Hulse (a man whose poppy shirt I own after winning it in the club raffle after the Portsmouth game, and whose poppy shirt I really wish I didn't own, as he was having a stinker of a season and I could well have done something better with my £200) opened the scoring as early as the 4th minute and for once it looked like we would actually do what a top side should do against a bottom side, and win handsomely.

Of course, nothing else happened until the second half, when Adel Taarabt once again showed his class with a brace, and although Preston found a late consolation, the R's saw it through and returned victorious once more to the summit of the Championship.

Baadiff (H)

November ended with a top of the table clash against our closest rivals Baadiff at Loftus Road. I knew this was an important one, as the message boards got wind that the game would be available somewhere on a stream. I spent my customary last ten minutes before kick-off desperately trying to find the game somewhere, and again had to make do with my commentary in Swahili.

Rangers fell behind after a quarter of an hour, when Kaspars Gorkss's cock-up in the centre of the pitch allowed Craig Bellamy, everyone's 'favourite' player, to fire at Paddy Kenny with enough force to see the visitors go in front. My computer desk took one hell of a clenched fist, I can tell you, while I'm sure even some of the residents of the nearby old people's home heard me scream "TW*T!!!!", nicely summing up my momentary falling out of love with our Latvian defender, a man I had previously had the pleasure of walking down South Africa Road with, alongside Joe and Queenie, after a *Sponsors' Evening*. Gorkss was charming, a complete gentleman and a credit to the club, in contrast to what we pretty much all think when we see Craig Bellamy, as emanating so eloquently from my potty mouth. Like any player who has ballsed up, Gorkss endeavoured to atone for his earlier blunder and righteously succeeded just a few minutes later, powering a header in that sent the home crowd wild. Indeed, I was so excited that I had to take a lie down in a semi-darkened room with a couple of *Kalms* and a glass of flat *7Up*.

The game was as tight as a duck's arse, until a moment of magic by guess who (yes, the mercurial Moroccan again), as he weaved his way through the Baadiff defence before curling a left foot shot into the top corner, which saw the R's in front and me shouting my head off, accompanied by not only the kids, but the current Mrs. Hartman too, in a chorus of "Da da da da da HOOPS! Da da da da da da da da HOOPS!!!!". It was compulsive viewing, as this win would mean we extended our lead at the top of the table to five points, AND we would be unbeaten in nineteen matches. When the final whistle came, the joy was overwhelming, and the conversation with Queenie that night was all about the match – a famous win that saw us go into December on a mega high.

We had not enjoyed such a great victory against the Welsh side since we had scored in the last minute at the old Ninian Park, when the late Ray Jones 'the teenager' had popped up with the winner that night. Who knows what Ray could have achieved had he not been so tragically taken from us in a car crash, aged just eighteen.

Watford (H)

And so, to league game number twenty of the campaign, and now people were starting to take notice. This match saw us up against Watford, live in front of the *BBC* cameras. I sat in my living room, with the luxury of my 50 inch HD screen to watch what I hoped would be the record-breaking match of all time play out. Sadly it wasn't to be. I could sit here and tell you that Watford were good and far outplayed us on the night. I could, but I won't. I will sit here as a bitter and twisted middle-aged man and say that we were pony and were lucky to score one (courtesy of Tommy Smith).

Leeds (A)

Still, we could get this minor blip out of our system and turn it on against Leeds at Elland Road. We could, but we didn't, and lost 2-0, and I am not going to dwell on this one either; suffice to say that I wasn't happy, and kicked the cat rather hard that evening, which I know wasn't the thing to do, especially as it's not our cat. No 'Posnan' celebration for me today, well, it was of sorts. I turned my back to the PC in disgust and jumped up and down – in rage!

Swansea (H)

Well, a Merry Christmas was had by one and all, and so, back to the football, on Boxing Day. Had the players stayed off the mulled wine and mince pies? Or were we in for our third stuffing on the bounce?

Swansea City came to the capital to try and inflict that third defeat on the spin, but it was the R's who took the lead, through Mackie's strike from Taarabt's assist, before Clint Hill and Alan Tate decided to live up to the boxing element of the day, both receiving the one card you really don't want to receive at this time of the year from the ref. Taarabt again caused havoc in the box and was felled by Ashley Williams, with Helguson notching the second goal of the game.

The second half belonged to Rangers and Adel, scoring the third, but saving the very best for last. Firstly he back-heeled the ball away from a Swansea player, and when he received the ball back he nutmegged Joe Allen, who gave up in shame, allowing Adel to run on and smash a brilliant strike in off the post, celebrated with a run towards the Loft end.

I had text updates for this one as we were round the mother-in-law's for our customary Boxing Day feast, where it seemed like my phone wasn't going to stop bleeping at me. When goals are going in I really don't mind, and I have to say this really made my Christmas, seeing us lead the division by four points with a plus twenty-six goal difference. With just one more game before the end of 2010, we were optimistic we could end the year on a high, and it was off to the Ricoh Arena for the R's next match, against an improving Coventry City, a game which again had caught the imagination of *Sky TV*, with a lunchtime kick-off.

Coventry (A)

In our green and white kit we really put on a show, playing our football and always looking dangerous. After a goalless first half, Kyle Walker surged down the right flank, and his cross shot went in off the Sky Blues' goalie Keiron Westwood. Cue choruses of "Jingle Bells, Jingle bells, jingle all the way, oh what fun it is to see Rangers win away - hay!" and that was just me in my living room.

With a third of the match remaining, Rangers scored again, Adel flighting in a beautiful ball for Tommy Smith to nod home and that really was that. So the year ended on a real high: with twenty-three games played, we now had a goal difference of plus twenty-eight, only having lost twice, and led the table by an impressive seven points. All we had to do was replicate that form for the second half of the season and we really would be home and hosed!

Norwich (A)

A happy new year it would have been, had we not played Norwich City at Carrow Road and forgotten to turn up. If I had just one opportunity to wish we'd played the way we had for much of the first half of the season, then today would have been that day. In reality, it looked like most of the side had been out the night before in the 'fine city' of Norwich, necking ale and chatting up cheap floozies (lucky beggars), while singing *Auld Lang Syne* (my dear) along Prince of Wales Road until the wee small hours, when they should have been getting some shut eye and putting their lives on the line to ensure we didn't lose this match at ANY cost.

Queenie had travelled up on the eve, as it was easier for him to fall asleep at my gaff than his own. So 'the three amigos' made the short trip to the match, stocking up on some pre-match fuel at the nearby *KFC*. The place was a sea of yellow and green and in my paranoia I felt all eyes were on us, the only Hoops in situ, although it was more likely due to the fact that I had much of the Colonel's secret recipe around my chops and dripping down my chin. Anyone from the opposition even daring to speak to me that day was likely to be decapitated by a stray drumstick!

I won't dwell on the game, as in truth there was little I can remember, having blocked most of it out thanks to ongoing therapy. I do recall there was a goal in it and us receiving yet another red card for Connolly (yes, we have been here before) for allegedly hauling down Grant Holt (yes, we have been here before also), although the alleged tug didn't even see a crease in his shirt. I'm sure a more believable story would have been:

a. a sniper got him, or
b. a blade of grass came up and took him out.

At the final whistle I remained positive, as we were still four points clear of our nearest rivals, Swansea City, and we had a game in hand.

This wasn't the first time that Queenie had attended a Norwich match; indeed, it had become a bit of an annual pilgrimage to watch the Boys turn out against my nemesis Norwich City FC. As such, he had become friends with my own mum and dad, who welcomed him like a long lost son. He was always respectful of their age and experience, and he loved to listen to my dad retell his stories from his colourful past. Mum would always greet him with the usual false disdain she saved for everyone.

"Oh, not you again! No, we don't want none!" as he knocked on the door of their mobile home. Just then she would swing the door open and announce "Get in here, you're making the place look untidy!", and in he would walk, larger than life, and plonk himself down on the sofa. Dad would be quick to pour him a drink, although he didn't really partake, but often would, just out of courtesy and not wishing to offend. It didn't take long for the stories to commence, Dad predominantly with his gangster yarns, and Queenie with the state of London's roads these days, and how Derrick was well shot of it. Mum would always put the kettle on for the obligatory cup of 'cha' and you could always be guaranteed a few laughs along the way, as the banter and 'slating' would commence as soon as he arrived.

Of all my friends, I think Queenie was one of Mum and Dad's favourites, not that they would ever admit to having such a thing, but perhaps it was due to the fact that they didn't see him that often, so his visits were kind of special and he was always polite and courteous. He was also a Londoner and our senses of humour all seemed to complement each other. I know that he was very fond of them as well; calling my dad 'Del Boy' and my mum 'Bezza' – the fact that they didn't bat an eyelid at such names meant that they saw him as a friend. And my parents, being fiercely protective of me, knew that I too was very fond of the great galah.

Our games against City over the years have seen mixed results. I won't be dwelling on the defeats here (for obvious reasons) but one that did stick in the craw was when we led 2-0, but allowed the home side back into it with woeful goalkeeping and park defending (although that would be unfair to park players perhaps), for them to win 3-2. Queenie knew how much I hated us losing to the 'Carrot' as he affectionately called them, as I had to live with that smugness, while he had seen us lose all over the place, so for him it was fairly routine.

On the plus side, I have also seen a few memorable wins down the years, my favourite was probably pre-Queenie, when I went with Mum and Dad to watch us edge a seven goal thriller, with a Rangers legend (although in many respects for all the wrong reasons) Devon 'Bruno' White grabbing Rangers' all important fourth. Chants of "Bruno, Bruno" reverberated around the tin stand as the big man took a bow right in front of us. I do also remember going to a *Zenith Data Systems Cup* match at Carrow Road (only because it was local and tickets were in plentiful supply!). On a bitterly cold evening, Rangers ran out worthy 2-1 winners: having taken the lead through Andy Sinton, the Canaries pegged us back to 1-1, before Andy Impey popped up in extra time to secure our passage forward in the competition. On another occasion, I was listening to a radio in the gents' toilets at work and heard us win 1-0 with a late Dennis Bailey goal!

More recently we managed a great 1-0 win, courtesy of a Martin Rowland's free kick, after having to hold on for the entire second half with 10 men, on account of Matt Connelly chopping an opposition player in half right under the ref's nose. Never a sensible move at the best of times! As the final whistle went, it was a feeling of absolute joy, yet for such a simple, and in many ways, insignificant victory. But as any fan will tell you, there are few games that are truly insignificant. When the team pull on your shirt, they take all your hopes, fears, aspirations and frustrations onto the pitch. I hoisted Joe up and gave him a big hug, and said "Yeeeeessssss, we WON!!!!" We applauded the team off at the end and chanted "The R's are going up". All a little premature as we were only a few games in, but I was happy to go along with that sentiment, caught up in the moment of having just beaten my 'old enemy'.

As we filtered out, I remember having a smile as big as the proverbial Cheshire Cat! Outside the ground, we were interviewed by two guys making a programme about the state of the club and what we as fans thought of things so far this season. I couldn't help but be 100% optimistic, having just secured three points, but the more far-reaching question was did we think the club were going in the right direction with the new ownership in place? In all honesty, I think if he had asked for my pin number and bank card I would have said 'yes', I was that happy that night!

However, I was brought back to reality from my brief trip down memory lane as I traipsed out of the ground, receiving a few text messages from jubilant Canaries, which I of course returned in good spirit, along the lines of "F*** off". I hoped that, as the saying goes, 'revenge is a dish best served cold' and that I would have the last laugh, come the end of the season.

Bristol City (H)

Two days later we had the chance to put that unlucky defeat behind us, with a home match against Bristol City. This was another match I had to endure on *Player*, interspersed with texts from Queenie. As if that wasn't bad enough, City actually had the audacity to take the lead, until Alejandro Faurlin restored parity and my heart rate to normal (so my office door remained safely on its hinges for now). Five minutes to go and I was straight out of the wheelie chair when my prayers were answered, Adel converting his spot kick – just what we needed after the injustice of two days earlier. But then disaster struck. OK, not on a titanic scale, but still. City levelled with the last attack of the game! Quite how my desk didn't snap in two with the force of my fist (or indeed my neighbour's eardrums weren't perforated when I exclaimed "SH*T!!!!") I will never know. But for all of this, the table showed we still commanded a five point lead at the top, although we now had the 'Carrot' sitting behind us in the second berth.

Blackburn Rovers (A)

Now, whilst I am not one for clichés, our next game was most certainly a 'welcome distraction' from the pressures of the 'bread and butter' league campaign, as we headed off to Ewood Park to play Blackburn Rovers in the FA Cup third round, sponsored by *E-on* (such is the power of sponsorship, you feel kind of compelled to say the *E-on* bit). Rangers fielded a below strength side – you could almost hear Neil Warnock saying it was so we could "concentrate on the league".

Ironically I was at Carrow Road that day, not due to any sudden change in allegiance, you will be pleased to hear, but the Canaries' third round FA Cup tie (sponsored by *E-on* - see, once you say it, it's like popping a *Pringle* - once you pop, you just can't stop) was against Leyton Orient, who just so happened to be Queenie's second team. As they are the minnows of League One and underdogs, I felt it only right to go along and shout as loudly as I could for anyone not playing in yellow and green that day. So we all went, and it was Katie's first ever match. She had been asking to come to a game, and I was a bit reluctant to take her all the way to West London: a long way if she didn't like it, and leaving her chained to railings until 16.55 seemed a tad cruel. So this seemed the perfect match for her baptism to football, allowing me to show her who we NEVER support and, conversely, that we pretty much support ANY other team playing against Norwich (although that would be put to the test if they played Chelsea, in which case the best I could wish for is a goalless draw with no shots on target and both sets of fans going home miserable and bewildered in equal measure).

We took our place with the travelling O's fans and it was great to see the match as an Orient fan for the day. I still wished I was at Ewood, but the thought of a near 400 miles round trip appealed as much as a root canal. The game was frenetic, the O's seeing this as a cup final in itself, with Norwich just looking to get the predicted home win and move into the draw for round four. Then a cross came in from one of the eleven heroes from Orient and QPR old boy Jimmy Smith ascended like an Antarctic Cod (well, it was a little chilly) to head us in front!

"YYYYYYYYEEEEEEEESSSSSSSS!!!!" I picked up Katie and we jumped up and down, as did Joe and even Kerri, along with around two thousand other O's fans. The songs began, the atmosphere electrifying as the O's sensed an upset was on the cards.

Into the second half and the O's were hanging on a bit, but defending well and looked surprisingly comfortable. With every tick of the clock, the fans around me became more tense, and I could sense in them the exact feeling I get when watching Rangers, how when it's this close to a victory (and an unlikely one especially) you just want that whistle to go, not least for the outpouring of emotion that follows. The away crowd's whistling was almost deafening and when the ref's actual whistle went, the cheer was tremendous. You genuinely felt the hairs on the back of your neck stick up (if only the hairs on my bald pate could grow back and do the same, I would have found an unlikely, but lucrative, cure to baldness).

I watched people hugging, kissing, back-patting – all the things you do when your team have just upset the form book – and my thoughts turned to the R's. As we filtered out, the announcer confirmed a 1-0 win for Rovers, so no shame against Premier League opposition. A funny old game, and with Orient scoring in the first and Blackburn in the second, it really was a game of two halves (but like I say I don't like to use such clichés, so of course these will all be edited out before the final book goes to print. Coughs).

Apart from being out of the FA Cup (sponsored by *E-on*) the only notable event was the loss of Jamie Mackie with a suspected broken leg. Much was reported on this, as Rovers' weasely front man, the much hated (by everyone, even Rovers fans) El Haj Diouf, had stood over Mackie and taunted him with comments that he was faking it. The sight of Mackie's leg hanging off didn't seem to deter him from making scurrilous accusations that Mackie should give up the great game and look for a part in the next Guy Ritchie movie. Afterwards, Neil Warnock came out and declared Diouf a "sewer rat", but later retracted the statement on advice from the club, after a small faction of sewer rats were said to be gunning for him, not wanting to be associated with Diouf as representative of them in any way, shape or form.

Burnley (A)

After the unwelcome distraction of the FA Cup third round (sponsored by... you get the idea), it was back to the bread and butter (and that one too) of the Championship, and a trip to Burnley, themselves still harbouring the belief that a playoff place was within their grasp. Burnley was the site of another great trip some years previously as part of the 'lads away day'.

Our average weight must have been a good twenty stones, so I felt positively lithe, relative to the rest of our group. Queenie endeared himself to the locals by humming the theme tune to the old *Hovis* advert as we walked through the cobbled Burnley streets. Whenever you were out walking with HRH and he eyed doggie do on the pavement he would always forewarn you by loudly exclaiming "Mind the Chelsea". And there we were, trying to look inconspicuous among the local stronghold, or at least, as inconspicuous as is possible for five blokes who can make a blot on the landscape that is the Lancashire hills. It was another rotten day out, football-wise with an almost expected and obligatory 2-1 defeat, but the 'craic' was excellent as always.

Anyway, up against us today was former R's favourite Clarke Carlisle, whose much publicised off-field liking for a bevvy or twelve and his understandable need to be closer to family up north were the catalysts for his move away to join Leeds. Not quite so understandable was his move a season later to Watford - not just because it isn't really classed as 'north' (although our readers in Penzance may disagree) but because it's Watford. I mean! Watford! And Carlisle was actually a half-decent centre half.

As the final score of 0-0 might suggest, this wasn't a classic either, so a point and no goals conceded were pretty much the highlights for statisticians and pundits to take away and analyse for minutes to come.

Coventry (H)

Sky's new found love for the league leaders was in evidence again, as Coventry City were our televised opponents for the second time. Having already beaten them 2-0 earlier in the season at the Ricoh, surely we could repeat the feat at Loftus Road and secure the much needed three points? I tried to stay focused on that fact, but my mind kept meandering off to the match in 1996, when we simply had to win to have any chance of remaining in the Premier League, and in spite of a massive following that day, were defeated 1-0, effectively relinquishing our right to stay up. Not that it was the worst place I have ever been before (I mean groundwise – as a place it ain't Buck House), as I have seen Rangers win there and go TOP of the league, but it is so long ago that the photos from the match are in sepia.

Today, Coventry boasted a man who inspired almost as much loathing as Diouf, in the form of Marlon King, a half-decent striker but zero decent human being, with convictions for, among other things, assault, receiving stolen goods, criminal damage, and numerous driving offences, so it was almost scripted that, for all the booing the home faithful gave him, it was he who opened the scoring for the Sky Blues. Not to be outdone, just before the break Adel Taarabt came weaving through the back line to curl a superb goal and take it to 1-1 at half time.

After much shouting at my plasma in the second half (which seemed to do the trick), and with literally one of the greatest passes I have ever seen from Adel (a full forty yard ball from the far touchline with the outside of his boot on the proverbial sixpence, to the on-running, returning for his second spell at the club, Wayne Routledge), his neat first touch and left foot finish found its way into the bottom right hand corner of the net. Routledge's run into the Loft faithful was greeted with much jubilation, and I was somewhat pleased (understatement). I opened my living room window to share my joy with (and scare) a few neighbours, with a tumultuous cry of...

"YYYYYYYYYEEEEEEEESSSSSSSSS!!!!"

...at the top of my voice, followed by a few choruses of "Da da da da HOOPS!" for good measure.

With Norwich and Baadiff both winning the day before, this was a much needed victory and maintained our five point lead at the top of the table.

Hull (A)

Next up, Dull, er, I mean Hull City. A 0-0 scoreline here reflects that a point gained is better than no points at all, and we stayed five clear at the top. This was one of those games where our 'talisman' Adel Taarabt threw not only his toys, but an entire aisle full of *Toys 'R' Us* exclusives out of the pram as well. This certainly proved to be a high spot as I don't remember jumping out of my wheelie chair once, nor breaking my knuckles on the office door and the imaginary feline stayed safely unkicked too. However, I do remember wishing I had a can of emulsion and an internal wall in need of a lick of paint, thus enabling me to watch it dry and at least give my life some purpose and meaningfulness, compared to what I had endured for the previous ninety minutes.

Pompey (H)

February 1st, and an evening game against Portsmouth, just as the away match had been earlier in the campaign. Another chance to sit at the PC, listening on *Player*, nursing a generous cheap scotch and *Coke*, and praying for three points. From where I was sat, Pompey seemed to be making more than a game of this one, and it sounded as tense as the previous encounter.

However in the second half, Adel yet again reminded us why he is so highly regarded, by striking the ball home to send us all into raptures. Joe was watching something behind me on the TV and my leaping up nearly sent him through the window, such was its ferocity!

After a few gulps of *Morrison's* 'finest for a tenner', I calmed down somewhat, until, unbelievably, I heard the words 'Clint', 'Hill' and 'Goal' in the same sentence! Now when something like this happens, particularly when you aren't actually witnessing it with your own eyes, you tend to stand transfixed, awaiting further confirmation that the commentators' area hasn't been infiltrated by a Chelsea fan hell-bent on messing with your head and subsequently messing up your night. Then I heard the crowd cheering and the confirmation came that it was indeed Hill who had scored.

"YES! GET IN!!!!" I shouted, as is customary, waving clenched fists in the air.

"Who scored?" Joe asked, his concentration thrown by my antics. I almost wanted to make up a more renowned scorer.

"Have a guess."

"Taarabt?"

"Nope."

"Helguson?"

"Nope."

"Miller?"

"Nope."

"Smith?"

"Nope, not playing."

"Give up."

"HILL!"

He looked at me like he does when I ask him to read or tidy his room; parents will know that look, a sort of mixture of disbelief and despair. But, with other teams around us also winning, Hill (incredibly) had helped to secure a vital three points for the R's (not the first time I have said that and it won't be the last).

Reading (A)

Just three days later, and The R's, with their new fans *Sky* in tow, headed off for our away return with the fake hoops of Reading. I of course was in my front seat position to enjoy the match in HD, joined by the whole Hartman clan of Joe, Katie and Kerri, as even the latter was starting to see that this season really could end on a magical note, and she wouldn't have to put up with the normal middle-aged, hormonal man for once (but perhaps just a middle-aged, slightly happier with his lot man). We seemed to be playing OK, but as the first half was drawing to a close, Hogan Ephraim decided to lunge in on Kebe, my analysis:

"It's a booking," followed by...

"It was a fifty/fifty challenge," leading to the realisation...

"Oh s***, it's red," and then...

"YOU STUPID TW*T!!!!"

You never want to lose a man when there's half a match still to play, and tonight was no exception. Rangers came out after the break and seemed to want to take the game to Reading; as the half wore on we still appeared to have the upper hand, even with the deficit in numbers. The clock ticked into the last eight minutes and Adel fed Ali Faurlin, who threaded a beautiful ball through to Routledge. As soon as I saw him striding through, I was up off my leather sofa (no significance in it being leather, but it describes the sofa better and fills up another few words, for the purposes of NaNoWriMo (see end credits). Hang on: it's actually an ageing, reddy brown leather sofa. There, that's better). Anyway, I was up off it and screaming at the telly:

"GO ON WAYNE!!!!" and as he bore down on goal, he was still ahead of his man.

"GO ON WAYNE!!!!" to the edge of the eighteen yard box.

"GO ON WAYNE, HIT IT!!!!"

And he did, across Adam Federici, away from his outstretched right arm, and into the far corner of the net!

"YYYYYYYYEEEEEEEESSSSSSSSS!!!! GET IN!!!! GET IN!!!!!!!!"

I puffed out my chest with immense pride for the ten men who had come to Reading (themselves just outside the play offs), kept going and taken a deserved lead. We just had to hold it now, and we did!

On the final whistle, I could have kissed the TV in absolute delight, and waited to see the league table, almost having to pinch myself to be sure that we really did still lead the Championship - by EIGHT points at this stage! It was the stuff of dreams, certainly mine for about the last thirty years. Well that and the one where Cheryl Cole and I are washed up on a deserted beach with only a pack of *Uno* cards for company and, well anyway, onto Forest...

Forest (H)

And the *Sky* love-in continued nine days later, when we entertained Nottingham Forest at the Rangers Stadium. Forest were the form team coming into the game, having won something ridiculous like forty matches on the spin (OK, OK, I have embellished this for the purpose of humour and trying to tell you they were doing pretty well, despite Billy Davies constantly moaning about needing more money to strengthen the side).

This was always going to be close: Rangers took the lead with a lovely strike from Tommy Smith and then about ten minutes later, Forest's Majewski, who forgot he was on a football field and not at the kick-boxing, lunged at Taarabt two footed, and saw a deserved red (don't you always find when it's the oppo it's 'deserved' and when it's your own man it's a 'fifty/fifty'?).

It seemed that this too could be a good day at the office. However, our luck ran out when a heavily deflected free kick from the visitors saw them level, and that's how it remained, with the spoils shared. "A good point" was how Warnock saw it, although I'm sure most R's fans failed to echo the manager's sentiments, along with "should have been three against ten men".

The other saving grace was that we didn't have to endure one of the ugliest footballers in British football history, as Rob Earnshaw remained an unused sub for Forest (or that's what the papers reported). My theory is he was away on international duty representing an Ugly Eleven V the Rest of the World. For those of you into your teams, this is how they lined up (allegedly):

The 'hit with the ugly stick' eleven...

1. Steve Ogrizovic
2. Gary Neville
3. Phil Neville
4. Martin Keown
5. Rio Ferdinand
6. Peter Beardsley
7. Jimmy Bullard
8. Iain Dowie
9. Luke Chadwick
10. Carlos Tevez
11. Robert Earnshaw

PNE (A)

So off to the potential banana skin under your foot of an already icy morning at Deepdale, home of the bottom side Preston North End. It had all the ingredients us R's fans have come to expect over the years: the expectation to win, a long trip up north, February, winter, against a team propping up the table, thus seeing this as a cup final and a last chance to beat anyone who mattered, before slipping down a division. However, it was Rangers who drew first blood, when Helguson put us 1-0 up. I called out to Joe, who was in the fields in front of our house playing football, held up one finger on my right hand (not the middle, if that's what you were thinking) and made a zero with the other forefinger and thumb.

"Helguson," I shouted.

Joe nodded and carried on with the far more important match with his mates. Everything seemed to be going to plan, but then I and the team remembered we were top and Preston were rock bottom. The inevitable equaliser rattled in. I guess in years past we would have gone on to lose two one, but this was a side made of sterner stuff, with their mind on the game and that ever useful point. That said, we couldn't beat the bottom team?

Ipswich (H)

Three days later and another evening match at HQ, where the Tractor Boys came to play. I have always had a bit of a soft spot for Ipswich Town; two reasons spring to mind. Firstly, they were bloody good back in the days when I started watching football. This was the Ipswich side of the early eighties, who won the UEFA cup under Bobby Robson, before I switched allegiance from Forest to Rangers, thus I considered them worthy adversaries, with the likes of Jon Wark, Paul Mariner, Eric Gates, George Burley, Kevin Beattie and Russell Osman, along with Paul Cooper in goal, who in one season saved eight of the ten penalties he faced, or something equally ridiculous. Secondly they were Norwich City's great rivals, so naturally I always back them. Thirdly (even though I said two reasons) they play in proper colours, and have a horse as a symbol, not a bird (OK, technically that's four so I am well over quota).

However, that was thirty years ago. Tonight I just wanted to smash them, just like every team we were going to face between now and the end of the season, or indeed anyone else who chanced to get between us and our destiny. After a tight and cagey affair in the first half (for 'tight' and 'cagey', read 'bugger all happened') it was that man Hill again who finally broke the deadlock and the Town fans' hearts (he didn't really, it's a figure of speech, more made them prematurely consider the train home). Once again, this correspondent went fair bonkers and was in danger of waking up the rest of the house (and possibly a few neighbours) in the process. The result was confirmed when a proper striker, in the form of Helguson, nodded in the second and that was that. Another game had been safely navigated and we still led by five points.

Middlesbrough (A)

February's last challenge saw the lads 'haway' to Middlesbrough, another team struggling at the wrong end of the table, and who on paper at least, we should turn over with some ease. For this one, I sat glued to *Player*, like a woman in labour to an entonox mask. Only that gives some relief (so I am told – not having delivered I can only go on the word of those who have), unlike *Player*, which only causes further pain, with frustrating gaps in commentary, or worse still, drops out completely.

As another close half drew to a close, Helguson struck first and we were on our way again. Then fifteen minutes into the second, Routledge got away from his marker and slung in the pinpoint cross for that man Helguson to nod home a beautiful second (and not a salmon or Antarctic Cod in sight), and send the R's faithful amassed behind the goal into ecstasy (although no drugs were taken in the making of this elation). I have watched this goal, as seen from the camera of a travelling R, and it is one of my favourites, where the sheer delight it captures totally sums up what it means to fans, who travel the length and breadth of the country, week in, week out, just waiting for away matches like this to unfold. The great day was capped when Taarabt was felled in the box. He got up, dusted himself down and coolly converted the penalty, giving us a resounding 3-0 victory, thus ensuring our five point gap remained and setting us up nicely for the visit a week later of another side still harbouring a playoff place: Leicester City, sitting in seventh place and seemingly in pole position.

Leicester (H)

So Mad March commenced with the visit of Leicester City, a game of such importance that rumour spread through the message boards that it was going to appear live on a stream. Whenever such a rumour goes round, there is a clamour for viable links for those too lazy/skint/busy (delete or add as applicable) to get to the match itself. There is always uncertainty as to who exactly is going to be showing the game, and you only know for sure you have found one that works about five minutes before kick-off, thus adding to the anxiety you are already feeling at this stage. My experience of streaming is that it can, and will, drop out at any time, but normally when you are on the attack, or about to take a dangerous free kick or corner, and the picture quality is ropey to say the least, but it sure as hell beats listening.

The game itself was very close, both sides enjoying chances and Paddy Kenny being called upon to make one or two great saves, particularly the one in the first half from Yakubu. The clock really did seem to be against us on this one, and with about five minutes left, Warnock replaced Taarabt with the on loan Ishmael Miller. Within two minutes of his arrival, Routledge played a ball up the line and into the big man's path. He raced free and left Foxes defender Bamba in his wake. Was this the moment? I was up out of the wheelie chair.

"Go on Ishmael. GO ON ISHMAEL. SHOOT!!!!"

He must have heard me, as at that point he let fly and the ball flew into the back of the net.

"YYYYYYYYEEEEEEEESSSSSSSSS!!!! GET IN!!!! GET IN!!!!!!!!"

The poor wheelie chair was sent hurtling backwards into the sofa and I, along with a packed Loftus Road, went mental!

To this day, one of my favourite *YouTube* clips is, again, from one of these guys in the crowd, who filmed the few seconds leading up to Miller letting fly, right through to the aftermath celebrations! The crowd's reaction is one of elation, mixed with visible relief that we had managed to sneak a win, in what looked like at best a draw. It also meant we opened up an eight point lead at the top of the table. Could we really dare to dream? Was this finally going to be it, the season we made it back to the Premiership, after sixteen long years? The next match, just three days later, against London rivals Millwall, would give us a chance to maintain or even strengthen our position.

Millwall (A)

Alas, it was one of those nights you wish to forget. I listened on *Player* with Joe, and from the sounds of it, we could easily have lost by a cricket score: anyone tuning in late could be forgiven for thinking it was the fifth day at Lords! 2-0 and the loss of big Dan Shittu with a red card was bad enough, but at least we could seek some solace, with Swansea only drawing, so our lead was still a healthy seven points.

So, thirty-six matches down, ten to go. If anyone had told me we'd be top at this stage of the season (or at any point of the season, for that matter) I would have driven them to the local asylum myself, and paid for private treatment out of my own account.

Crystal Palace (H)

Another London derby was to follow, against Crystal Palace, who themselves had the very real threat of relegation to contend with, so came to Loftus Road needing the win as much as we did. Another tortured afternoon of ears glued to *Player* was relaxed slightly when Helguson scored for the R's, only for the torment to return when Palarse equalised through Vaughan.

The second half sprang into action on fifty-three minutes when Adel was felled. For his efforts, McCarthy was awarded a red card and Rangers a penalty, which Helguson, the Icelandic hitman, converted into the Loft end and the R's were back in front two to one. Cue celebrations in my small cubic office and at HQ, where the chimes of "Da da da da HOOPS!!!!" could be heard from one hundred plus miles away (and no doubt from one hundred metres away by my neighbours in my small corner of Norfolk).

Thankfully that's how it remained, and with the results from the other games played that day, we led the division by a staggering ten points. Now with nine games remaining, all manner of mathematicians clambered out of the message board woodwork, with their speculations of "if we won X many games and [other rivals] lost X many games, we could be promoted by such and such a match". The truth was it was still way too early to tell, and the old cliché of 'take each game as it comes' was never more apt.

What was mathematically true was that if we won another seven games, we couldn't be caught at any rate, and we would be the champions. But it was hard not to look ahead to the last nine games of the season, and try to ascertain which games we should win, which we should draw, which we might lose and so on.

And there of course is the beauty of football. There are no givens, just as there are no givens in life: just as we can't predict scores and results of matches, we can't truly say what will happen on our own journey through life with any real authority. Having said that, with the record we had thus far and with only four defeats from thirty-seven matches, even the most pessimistic (i.e. nigh on all) Rangers fans would have been hard pushed to see more than a couple of defeats at most, between now and the end of the season.

One event that was simmering behind the scenes, and had been for a few months but was now gathering some momentum, concerned the irregularities surrounding the transfer of Rangers midfielder Alejandro Faurlin. This was to prove a growing concern to all at the club, as various scare stories seemed to be emanating from the message boards as to the severity of the charges the FA were in the process of bringing against us, and more importantly, the severity of punishment they could impose – anything from a hefty financial fine to even, as was being touted, a possible points deduction. If the latter was possible, then the lead we had amassed over our nearest rivals may yet still prove to be in vain. All we as fans could hope for was that we were actually innocent of any charges the FA may bring, or, if we were found guilty of any wrongdoing, then some leniency on the sanctions imposed and a good lawyer to fight our corner!

Doncaster (A)

Our attentions turned again to the one area we could control, which was back on the pitch, and our next challengers, Doncaster Rovers. As you started to consider the final few matches in more detail, you really did find yourself looking at games and not only wondering how many points you may get from it, but also who your nearest rivals were playing and what points they may pick up. You found yourself becoming a 'fan for the day' of any team playing Baadiff, Swansea or Norwich, sometimes almost losing sight of the fact that your destiny is in your own hands.

The other factor you consider is what's in it for the other team? What do they still have to play for? In the case of Donny, not much. Whilst not completely and mathematically safe from relegation, it was unlikely they could go down, so perhaps the old professional pride and getting one over on the league leaders and Champions Elect would make this tougher than it needed to be, in which case we wouldn't be seeing the three points undoubtedly already earmarked, by management and supporters alike.

After an uneventful first forty-five, Rangers livened up proceedings early doors, and Hogan Ephraim, overlooked for much of the season, rounded off a fine pass from Wayne Routledge, to curl a beauty into the bottom corner. 1-0 and much merriment all round!

I don't remember too much more of note, as 1-0 is where it

stayed, nonetheless ensuring a nine point gap remained between us and our now nearest rivals Norwich. Thus a largely satisfying March (with the exception of the blip at the office called Millwall) came to a close and set up a hugely important April for all associated with the club.

Sheffield United (H)

Monday 4th April saw the first of seven games that would surely decide the fate of Queens Park Rangers Football Club and determine, after sixteen long years out of the top flight of English football, whether promotion would finally be ours. Sheffield United were next up at Loftus Road, and they really were a club with something to play for, themselves ensconced in a relegation battle which saw them top of the bottom three, with Preston and Scunthorpe beneath them, but some seven points adrift of the last safe spot, currently occupied by Crystal Palace. While I don't like to see any side relegated, as I know only too well the turmoil the real fans, young and old alike, go through – an often long and lingering demise throughout the season that sometimes is only confirmed on the last day – I have always had a soft spot for the London sides (with the exception of Chelscum, who due to location and my football upbringing will always be our bitterest and most detested rivals, along with Norwich: the 'irrational hate' team we are all entitled to).

So, with that in mind, and the fact that our need was greater, a repeat of our earlier cutting down to size of the Blades was quite alright in my book. Another night glued to the *Mac* and the delights of *QPR Player* then, and on the half hour the deadlock was broken through Routledge, himself proving to be an inspired loan signing from Newcastle. Much belief (and relief, I have to say) that this was going to be three points, and so it proved, with Faurlin adding a second early after the break and that man Routledge wrapping it up with a third. With Norwich also winning again, the gap remained at nine points.

Scunthorpe (A)

The phrase 'banana skin' could have been invented for games like our next encounter, to rock bottom of the table and seemingly all but relegated Scunthorpe United. If ever you were going to put your proverbial house and last remaining *Rocha.John Rocha* shirt on the outcome of a match in Rangers favour, then now was the time to do so. With twenty-two places, forty-four points and a staggering sixty-six goal difference separating the two sides, even the most pessimistic of Rangers fans couldn't really see anything other than a handsome victory for the R's. And it started brightly, forgotten man Rob Hulse scoring as early as the seventh minute and getting the early party celebrations underway.

Needless to say, and with the way I have built this up, what followed took the form book and not only rewrote it, but shredded it, burnt it and scattered the ashes all over Glanford Park. Despite having other chances to extend the lead, we didn't capitalise and it was Scunny who equalised in the first half. Where we had so often come out of the blocks so well in the second half, this was to be our worst performance result-wise of the entire season, completely capitulating and conceding a further three second half goals.

Still, every cloud has a silver lining, as they say, so with Norwich also losing, the result had no effect whatsoever on the table or points standings, although what effect it may have had on morale and belief only time would tell, for this day belonged to United, who lifted themselves off the bottom of the Championship with hope, albeit feint, that they could still avoid the drop.

Barnsley (A)

A response was needed, and we got the chance to put the Scunny debacle to bed (hopefully pulling the thirteen tog quilt right up over our heads and never letting that result see the light of day again), with a trip to Barnsley. Much as I wanted to sit stone-faced and half crapping myself in front of *Player*, I was actually on a rare night out, watching eighties faves, Big

Country's reformed line-up belt out their greatest hits at the Norwich Waterfront. While I have always loved the group and I have seen them more than most over the years, my thoughts were at Oakwell. I had asked Queenie to provide me with text 'apples' throughout the night, as he was going to be listening in with enough intensity for the both of us.

At every given opportunity, I checked my phone - kick-off was at 7.45pm, and I impatiently awaited the first text, literally praying for it to be a favourable one. My phone vibrated at 7.46pm, during a rather fine rendition of *Fields Of Fire*, and my heart skipped a beat. Rangers had scored after forty-seven seconds through Adel Taarabt! I punched the air in time to the music and nearly hit the guy standing just that little bit too close to me! Unfortunately Queenie was in one of those moods where he would send texts every few minutes with any kind of update, from a free kick or substitution, to scores from the other games in the Championship that night. This was great in one way, to be kept abreast of everything going on, but also a terrible idea, as I dreaded every vibration and subsequent text be the one that said "1-1".

As much as I tried to enjoy the evening, the constant vibrating was a major distraction, and it didn't help I was standing quite near the front of the venue, with the sound amplification going right through me, having only recently got over a nasty bout of bronchitis. The 'BOOM, BOOM, BOOM' of the speakers nearly lifted me off my feet, so what, with the thumping of the beat boxes and the vibration of my mobile, I was fast becoming a nervous wreck. I had estimated that, even with stoppages, the game would be up by 21.40 at the latest. However, about ten minutes before that, the texts dried up. My vivid imagination was now imagining all sorts. Barnsley have scored two late goals, I thought, and Queenie's gone out on the rampage in Chingford, asking people what team they support, and decking them if they give the wrong answer. I found myself frantic with the not knowing, texting him in desperation to try and establish if the game had actually finished or not.

The text back said "playing five minutes of injury time!", enough to send my high blood pressure off on another wave of

180 over 120. When the next text came through I had calculated only about four minutes had lapsed, and I tried to convince myself that they had scored a last gasp equaliser, just as they had all those years ago when we went on the lads' away trip.

I almost couldn't open the text, partly in fear of what it was going to say, partly as one of my friends had just bought another drink and I couldn't hold a pint in one hand and open the text with the other. When I finally saw it, it read "FT 0-1".

"YES!!!!" I exclaimed, perhaps a little loudly, as it was audible over a five-hundred-strong audience and a rousing rendition of *In A Big Country*. Finally I could relax and enjoy the rest of the gig and a few (i.e. lots) more ales.

Derby (H)

Our next big match was at home to Derby and was again to be televised by our new friends at *Sky Sports*. I was going to be away from home again for this match, this time on a course with my new work venture, down in Swindon, of all places. I had been there once before to see Rangers many years previously, a dire affair back in the days when I went to such places on a rain-soaked midweek 'anything but' jolly, and can recall a rather painful 1-0 defeat, not untypical of a Rangers away day scoreline.

Throughout the first day of my course, and while trying to concentrate on all the new things I really did have to try and take in, I was constantly thinking of the match, in particular, how/where I was going to watch it. The hotel didn't seem to be advertising *Sky* in any way, shape or form, so on completion of the first day's play, I made my way back to check out who may be showing it. The pub across the road had that look of the sort of venue that would show live sports, while selling a mean pint of locally brewed ale, as well a cheap carvery on a Sunday. I ventured across and found it to be a kind of reverse TARDIS that looked quite spacious from the outside, but had a couple of snugs and very little else on the inside, other than one or two locals donning the kind of expression that said "Leave now while you still have a chance".

I ventured back to my car and followed the signs for Swindon Town Centre, taking the chance that I wouldn't end up going in ever decreasing circles on its infamous 'Magic Roundabout', never to be seen again. After about fifteen minutes, I found a boozer that again had that look about it that said "Come in and watch *Sky Sports* here", but without a sign that said as much. Optimistic, I parked up, but turned quickly on my heels when I saw a collection of the local Neanderthals converging outside. In desperation, I decided to head back to the hotel, left only with the option to await text updates from Queenie while I drank the optics dry. On arrival, I spotted a few of the other delegates, and we got chatting about the day, including my sampling the delights of Swindon whilst looking for a pub showing *Sky Sports*.

"Oh," someone said, "They show it here, you just have to ask."

This was like an alcoholic being told there was a free bar, so I immediately tracked down the restaurant manager, who agreed to sort it out. Only problem being he didn't stipulate which night, and my patience was running more than a little thin. So, after wolfing down my main course quicker than Usain Bolt walking his pet labrador, I chatted up the rather lovely looking barperson – lovely fellow – and he changed the channel.

And we were away! QPR v Derby, just five minutes in, and no score. As the half progressed, others from the course joined the table, and the beer flowed, unlike the football. The whole match seemed to be about Adel Taarabt v Robbie Savage, a man you either hated or really disliked. There was little in it and Derby probably had the best chance, but Kenny made a great save. In the end, with the place mostly deserted or asleep (some at the bar), the game was up at 0-0 – not a total disaster, as we still had an eight point lead, with just four matches to go, albeit that the next game promised to be one of the toughest of the lot, away to third placed Baadiff. But the prize couldn't be bigger, because a win could actually mean we were promoted, and, barring a mathematical catastrophe, as champions.

Cardiff (A)

So, it was with some excitement that Queenie and many thousands from West London travelled in hope and expectation, to see if we could finish the job in South Wales, at the inventively named Cardiff City Stadium. I was rooted to my leather sofa, to watch the game in HD, courtesy of the *BBC's* live coverage. Rangers were resplendent in green and white hoops, and the game was being played at a frenetic pace. After just six minutes, Jay Bothroyd picked the ball up on Rangers' left side, went on a mazy run that seemed to beat the entire team twice, before cracking a left footed strike into the top right hand corner of Kenny's goal, and in off the underside of the bar so hard I felt the vibrations in my own living room. Had it been against anybody other than us I would have been eulogising about it for many years to come. As it was against us, we'll move on.

Enter our own talisman in the form of Adel Taarabt. Just four minutes after Baadiff had fortuitously taken the lead, Adel popped up down our left side and curled an outrageous shot into the far top corner. 1-1, and as you may expect, the many thousands of Hoops fans there on the day, along with the many around the country watching on TV (myself included) went a touch mental! Game on!

Baadiff were like a wounded animal, and continued to break at us, at pace, and then with thirty-five on the clock, Craig Bellamy restored the Bluebirds' lead. 2-1, and that's how is stayed until half time.

So, Champagne on ice, and work to be done, and in the second half there were certainly signs that we could still get something out of the game. With twenty minutes to go, Routledge played the ball up to Taarabt, who controlled it instinctively, turned his marker, and scored brilliantly in the bottom right hand corner: 2-2! I was jumping round the living room like I had just re-checked my winning lottery numbers, and raced downstairs to shout to Joe, who was playing outside in the park.

Then it was back to the action. Was it greedy to want to see us do it now? Today? Rangers pressed forward, and in the dying moments, Helguson narrowly missed converting the perfect cross that would have seen us over the line with three games to spare. Even so, with all results in that day, we now had a seven point lead over Norwich and an eight point lead over Baadiff, so a win in our next game, just two days later on Bank Holiday Monday, against Dull City, would see us up, as champions.

Hull (H)

I had already managed to purchase tickets for not only myself, Joe and Katie (for what would be her first Rangers match), but also the current Mrs. Hartman, as it looked likely that this match could well decide our promotion and maybe even the Championship title itself. While I would have dearly loved to have seen us clinch promotion at Baadiff, there was also a bit of me that wanted to see it happen, live, in front of my very eyes, with my kids alongside me, and at Loftus Road, just to make the fairytale complete. We travelled down in the morning on the train as a family, with plenty of *Uno* to keep us company, as well as munching on our 'pack up' en route. We were met outside the ground by Queenie and Jim, and exchanged banter and predictions. It was really good to see them, resplendent in their home replica kits (albeit a somewhat snug fit since *Lotto's* involvement in manufacturing our tops – clearly there are no fat Italians). Joe and Katie matched their elders' efforts on the fashion front and raised the stakes with JOE 9 and KATIE 6 on the backs of their shirts.

We had seats in the Ellerslie Road stand, towards the away end, in a not dissimilar seat to that for the Norwich game, but I couldn't help but hope this wouldn't end a draw, although technically, even if Baadiff were to win today and we only got a point, we would be all but promoted. Well, this was actually a moot point, as a date for our FA hearing over the Faurlin transfer was now set, with much uncertainty as to whether we would be allowed to keep the points we had already amassed. However, we just needed to concentrate on winning this match, and leave the suits to decide what punishment, if any, should be awarded for our alleged shenanigans.

In front of a near full stadium, and on a super sunny day, it really looked like the gods were smiling down on us. Just moments before kick-off, the scoreboard always shows a compilation of great moments and great players from yesteryear. It reminds you how wonderful the club is, and what it means to so many to follow the R's. Such was the emotion of the day, the feeling that we could reach out and touch the Premier League again after so long. After so many ups and downs, and having the next generation sitting with me, it was a really emotional moment for me, and I felt tears of immense pride well up. I was brought back to reality by the tannoy announcement I had heard so many times before...

"Ladies and gentlemen. This is Loftus Road. We are QPR. Will you welcome Hull City and QUEENS. PARK. RANGERS!!!!"

...followed by the distinctive *Papa's Got A Brand New Pigbag*. When everyone is on song and Loftus Road is packed, there is nothing better than hearing a few bursts of "Da da da da HOOPS, da da da da da da da da HOOPS!!!!" to get everyone rocking! The atmosphere was electric; a sense of anticipation that today was the day, when (not quite) "thirty years of hurt never stopped me dreaming" – having supported the R's for that long (and a little bit more), the famous line from Baddiel and Skinner's *Three Lions* could well have been written for us.

Once kick-off was moments away, the crowds noise reached fever pitch, and we were away! The usual sparring was evident in the first few minutes as both sides tried to get a foothold. Then with nine minutes gone on the clock, Taarabt played a superb pass into the path of Wayne Routledge, who suddenly had the whole of the Dull half to run into. It was a surreal moment, as even though he was running full pelt into enemy territory and pulling away from his marker, the crowd's expectation suddenly rose, and faces seemed to freeze in the moment. Those around me, myself included, stood up, as Routledge was in shooting distance. Was this the moment?

"SHOOT WAYNE!!!!" And he did! A cracking right foot strike that hit the net, 1-0!!!!

"YYYYYYYYEEEEEEEESSSSSSSS!!!!!!!!"

The crowd went absolutely mental, the proverbial roof was lifted off Loftus Road, and I grabbed Katie, forgetting she had never witnessed anything quite like this (Orient scoring at Norwich aside) and lifted her up so she could see Routledge wheel away in delight and so we could all celebrate the moment with further chants of "DA DA DA DA HOOPS!!!! DA DA DA DA DA DA DA DA HOOPS!!!! DA DA DA DA DA DA DA DA HOOPS!!!!" Never had the chant been sung with such conviction, the utter relief and joy of knowing that we had witnessed the goal that could secure everything in one day. Today. All we had to do now was hold on for eighty-one minutes, easy!

Half time came, half the job done! The customary sweets and drinks came out for the kids, along with a toilet break, and then it was down to a nerve-wracking final forty-five, where history was hopefully in the making. As the half wore on, it was evident that the players were feeling the tension transcending from the stands, as they seemed to fall back deeper and deeper, a sure sign of being under immense pressure. Dull pressed forward, sensing our defensiveness, and not forgetting that a win for them with two games to go meant they still had a chance of sneaking into the playoffs. I found myself watching the scoreboard clock and willing the minutes away. It's at times like these you really feel inadequate, not dissimilar to how you feel as a man watching an adult movie. Not that I would know of course. (Coughs).

Then disaster struck on eighty-one minutes. A pass over the top of our defence and it was like Gary Neville had pressed the pause button on his *Sky* panel and frozen our back line and suddenly the ball was in: 1-1. Thoughts now turned to the other games featuring Norwich and Baadiff. How were they fairing? The amateur mathematicians in the crowd started to work out all the permutations. Never mind all that, we need a goal and not to concede another, simple enough for you?!

Although we managed the latter, we couldn't quite realise the former, and 1-1 was how it remained. As the referee's whistle blew, the crowds began to invade the pitch: as far as

186

they were concerned we had done enough, a point meaning we still had a six point cushion over Baadiff, now on seventy-nine points after their win was confirmed, but with a far superior goal difference. We were all but there.

And what of Norwich? The announcer said they were still playing, and were currently level. So that meant they had seventy-eight points as it stood, and third place. Then news hit a mobile behind me that the Canaries had scored late on in their match, which meant we definitely were NOT champions (at least for another week) AND we were definitely NOT mathematically promoted yet either. While many thousands had invaded the pitch, for the majority it certainly wasn't 'job done' just yet, and as we filed out of the ground and met up with Queenie again, there was a sense of dejection, that we had missed out on our fairytale ending.

Thoughts now turned to our penultimate match of the campaign, against Watford, one of the few sides to have beaten us already this season. If that wasn't bad enough, the pessimists among us also noted that if they did the unthinkable and completed an unwelcome double over us, our final match was at home to 'dirty' Leeds, who had (you guessed it) also beaten us back in 2010, a week before Christmas! Surely we couldn't have blown it this late in the day, having led the division for almost the entire campaign?

Maybe it wasn't the last two matches that would decide our fate anyway, as the court case loomed large, with all manner of speculation as to the number and severity of charges being prepared by the FA, and more worryingly, the extent of punishment that could be meted out. We would have to wait another week for that vital match at Watford, and then sit and hope we only got a rap on the knuckles from the FA, but only time would tell.

HRH and Jim v Hull

Watford (A)

Saturday 30th April, 2011: Rangers travelled to Vicarage Road, home of Watford, for the penultimate match of the 2010-2011 season. Today was finally the day when just one point would see us promoted, with a win securing the Championship, and all the hard work and dedication would prove to be worthwhile. I was unable to get tickets for the game, unsurprisingly, so it was left to the 'World Service', in the shape of Queenie himself, and a stream of the game, to see what I had waited so long to see, since the doom-ridden season of 1995-1996, and watching us beat West Ham 3-0 at Loftus Road in the final home match, only to find that other results had conspired against us, and we were relegated anyway. Queenie and I still travelled to Nottingham to watch Forest demolish us by the same scoreline a week later. Little did we realise that it was going to take sixteen long years to be on the brink of a return.

I found one of the many replica shirts I own (but one of the few that still fit me) and pulled it on, in the vain hope that it might make me feel that little bit closer to that small corner of

Hertfordshire, where I really wanted to be in body, but was more than there in spirit. Like an expectant father, I began nervously pacing the floor, yet still I had a nagging doubt about today – not the opposition or whether we could actually get a result or not, but over the impending court case and its likely outcome. Some papers were going to absolute extremes as to what punishment the FA could impose, ranging from a small fine to points deductions, some saying as much as fifteen points. I even read somewhere that we could even face expulsion from the league altogether.

While I couldn't see the latter, the points deduction did still seem a very real possibility, as so many people (none with any concrete evidence) were stating similar, on the message boards and in the press. Newspapers (and not all gutter press) ran stories with comparisons to the Tevez case years earlier. I tried to put this to one side, and hoped the players would too, as today, all that mattered was getting at least a draw from this match. Watford only had professional pride to play for, which suited us. Now we had to be professional ourselves one more time.

Not surprisingly the game was tense. Rangers were clearly the better footballing side, but couldn't get a goal to show for it. Half time came and went, and the nerves were truly jangling, the R's kicking towards their own fans, amassed to the right of the goal for the second period. I was up and down out of my wheelie chair, the tension almost unbearable. As it stood we were up, but you just had that dreadful feeling in the back of your head that Watford could grab a late goal and really upset the party. Then, with a lucky-for-some thirteen minutes remaining, Tommy Smith burst down our left side and centred. And there, as if to further confirm his newly awarded *Championship Player of the Season 2010-2011* accolade, Adel Taarabt flicked the ball into the far corner, and the place erupted! I leapt out of my chair and in doing so, kicked it backwards with such force I nearly broke the door frame!

"YYYYYYYYYYYYYEEEEEEEEEEESSSSSSSSSSSSS!!!! GET IN!!!! GET IN!!!!!!!! THAT'S THE ONE!!!!"

Such elation, such relief!!!! Surely we were on the way

now?! We just had to keep the ball, play our football, and not concede! See out the rest of the time. We could do this!

Time dragged, and when the board for added time went up there were still FIVE big minutes left! The tension was excruciating, when Tommy Smith again picked up the ball on our left, only this time cutting in and finishing with aplomb in the bottom left hand corner!

"YYYYYYYYYYYYYYYYYYYYYYYEEEEEEEEEEEEEE EEEEEESSSSSSSSSSSSSSSSSSSSSSSSSSS!!!!!!!!!!!!!!!!!!!!"

I ran out of my house, into the street, shouting to Joe, who was playing football himself.

"Mate! Mate!" I called. He came running over and immediately guessed something good had happened, as I was holding two fists aloft, with a smile like I had already witnessed the return of my beloved club to the big time.

"We're up mate!" is all I could say.

"We won?" said Joe.

"Well, winning two nil, but it's just about over."

I ran back into the house and there we were, plastered all over *Sky Sports*, with joyous scenes of Adel Taarabt, wrapped in a Moroccan flag, celebrating with the travelling R's faithful! Faurlin and Taarabt flanked Warnock, their smiles nearly as big as ours.

It was confirmed! We had won 2-0 and we were up as the Champions! I called Queenie to savour the atmosphere from Hertfordshire live, just as pleased for him, as I knew it meant as much, if not more to him, and he really deserved it too. He had put in the miles over the years, going home and away for many seasons, through tough times, and tougher times. I remember speaking to him live from Huddersfield in 2001 as we lost and I was telling him that not only were we losing there but we were also losing our, at the time, First Division status as well. We had been at the Millennium stadium together to see us miss out on a promotion back to the First Division in 2003. We had been there in 1999, needing a win to stay up, and somehow achieving it in our last game of the season against Palace, winning 6-0 to secure our status. We had watched as local rivals Chelsea had been bankrolled from mediocrity to Champions League contenders while we slipped into administration and nearly from existence. We had seen us reach rock bottom and have the ignominy of losing to non-league Vauxhall Motors in the FA Cup.

But somehow, all of the lows are necessary to make the rare days like today so much the sweeter. I thought of Mum, naturally. But there was still this terrible feeling that somehow, inexplicably, this was all just a dream and the nightmare part was about to begin, where everything was taken away from us – all the hard work by the players, the manager, the management team – the hopes of generations dashed. While the players celebrated vociferously in the away changing room after the match, I really couldn't fully celebrate that night, and in truth, neither could anyone else who truly cared about the club.

On the following Monday, two other games were to take place, involving our closest rivals. While Baadiff entertained Middlesbrough in the afternoon, Norwich were at Portsmouth in the evening, with both sides vying for the second automatic place behind Rangers, assuming of course we didn't face expulsion from the league and hand them both automatic places. I watched the Baadiff match, a game they had to win to put pressure on Norwich later, and send it to the last games of the season to decide everything. Incredibly, Boro won 3-0, which meant a win for Norwich and they would definitely be promoted. My neighbour, an armchair Canary, asked if he could watch the match at mine, and as I was going to be watching it anyway, I thought it the Christian thing to do (even though I'm not Christian). I thus had to endure watching Norwich win 1-0 and secure their promotion. So, while they were able to enjoy their moment and look forward to their last match of the season, at home, we Rangers fans, staff and players couldn't, for the impending court case was due to begin tomorrow.

The case was heard in full at Wembley Stadium, with *Sky Sports* covering the to-ing and fro-ing from FA officials, legal eagles and representatives of the club, including Alejandro Faurlin himself, the man at the centre of the third party ownership irregularities that, if the club had breached, would almost certainly lead to points being deducted and our title being take away. I was wandering around in the weirdest mood imaginable, elation tempered by the prospect of not actually even being promoted. I guess it was a feeling not dissimilar to winning the lottery and mislaying the ticket. I kept coming back to *Sky Sports News*, not a great idea as their chief football hack's pessimism increased exponentially each time he popped up, the impressive backdrop of Wembley Stadium behind him. I am convinced his suit got darker every time the cameras went back to him, and could even make out vultures flying overhead.

It then emerged that no decision was to be made until the following Monday, thus making the farce even greater. Did they really conceive that we would play our final match of the campaign on Saturday, against Leeds, not knowing the outcome of the court case? How could players prepare for a match when they didn't know if they should win, lose, draw or even bother turning up? I, like a lot of people that week, felt cheated. All season we had given our everything, only for it to come down to a non-playing football matter. Seven charges now hung over us, and as each day passed, the doom and gloom seemed to get worse.

That evening, Joe and I attended our third *Sponsors Night*, held at the W12club, having this season sponsored goalkeeper (and, as it transpired, both QPR's Players' and Supporters' Player of the Season) Paddy Kenny's gloves. A fine memento of a fabulous season, and a mighty fine pair I might add (of gloves I mean – certainly kept out many goals and kept his hands nice and warm in the winter too, I'll wager). Also in attendance was our honorary special guest HRH, who was, as was customary, late. It always fascinated me that Joe and I could make it all the way from Norwich in time, when Queenie only had to make it a few short miles across the capital. As usual the banter between us was good. I always threatened him with expulsion if he got too 'lairy', reminding him that he was only there as a special favour, and that I could have him escorted from the premises at any time! But with all the potential doom hanging over the club with the imminent FA decision, the event was really, well, a non-event. The players seemed unfocused and more distracted than in previous years, and we hardly had time to secure any photos or autographs at all.

Sponsors Nights are normally a great way to get 'up close and personal' with the players, most of whom didn't want to get up close and personal with us unfortunately. While meeting a player who has represented your club, and may even have reached legend status at some point, is an exciting moment for any fan of the team, the prospect of meeting some starry-eyed daydreamer hungry for an autograph (and I mean me here, not the kids) isn't that high on the professional footballer's bucket list of '100 things I need to do before I croak'. My first sponsorship evening was in 2009, and I remember looking at players and thinking "He's not that tall in real life", or "have a shave", and no, it wasn't Movember, so there was no excuse really. That first season we sponsored R's legend Lee Cook's away top, along with the most underused items ever (as he had been out virtually all season long with a serious injury) in Rowan Vine's shin guards. I remember when Joe and I went up to collect Cook's shirt, for some reason they couldn't find it initially (maybe my cheque hadn't cleared yet), so I jokingly said that if they couldn't find the replica one I would have the shirt he was wearing. I think he saw the funny side of this – either that, or he was smiling and laughing whilst frantically searching for security. Vine was quite miserable I recall, although quite a few of the other players, like Helguson and Ainsworth, were more than happy to have photos taken and to sign autographs. The others just played on their mobile phones all evening, presumably texting each other to say how much fun they were having, meeting the people who were ultimately responsible for them getting paid each week.

The second year we sponsored Akos Buzsaky's away shirt, and he was only too happy to talk afterwards, complaining how hot it was in the suite. He was hot! I was running around like a blue-arsed fly, trying to get two shirts signed and getting Joe into as many photo opportunities with players as possible!

193

This event seemed much better organised and the players more genuine, staying around for longer, allowing me to get autograph upon autograph. It was precisely the distraction I could have done with now, to keep my mind off the verdict and the potential consequences for the team I had loved all my adult life, enough to shell out the reddies year upon year and hang around players like a starstruck teenager at a stage door.

Leeds (H)

Joe and I had managed to get tickets for the final match, although we didn't know for sure why we were going! To celebrate? What? We didn't know if there was anything to celebrate! Then other teams started to raise the questions. If points were deducted, how did that affect the playoff semi-finals? Would QPR be involved in those? No-one knew, as nobody could say how many points would be deducted, if any were at all!

When Saturday finally came, Joe and I headed off to London on the train, for the 12.45 kick-off, still unaware of the FA's findings and final verdict. Today should have been one of the greatest in my footballing life, certainly Joe's best ever, and who knows, maybe the last ever great day. QPR are, at the end of the shift, one of the smaller teams in London's elite: we are never going to compete with the likes of Arsenal, Spurs and Chelsea, but what we lack in numbers, we always make up for in loyal support. It also means while the Man Uniteds of this world are used to winning trophy after trophy, it's not something QPR have ever been blessed with, and neither will they be, unless some mega-rich benefactor comes in and bankrolls the club. I for one wouldn't want that anyway; I would much rather see the club built up on solid foundations: a strong youth policy, a sensible budget that attracts good players, and for this steady rise to one day culminate in a cup success.

We arrived at London Liverpool Street in good time, and made our way across the city via the underground, a familiar trip, with Joe leading the way, decked out in replica shirts and still not knowing what the day had in store. We arrived at

White City station and took our normal 'nifty' shortcut through a housing estate, then back on to the main South Africa Road, following the hordes down to the ground. It was eerily quiet, considering a full house was expected, and this could only be due to the complete lack of belief that we had actually won promotion at all, that the last forty-five games had been a figment of our very overworked imaginations. As we approached The Springbok pub, I fumbled for my wallet so I could purchase a copy of the match programme, from a seller just beyond this landmark and just before the burger stand that I and, even more regularly, Queenie would frequent.

It was at this point that an almighty cheer went up from somewhere around the ground. Somewhat perplexed, I looked at Joe, and even found myself checking the time to see if we had arrived late and missed a goal. Just then I received a call from Nigel confirming a decision had been made and that there would be NO POINTS DEDUCTION! It seemed somehow apt that the man responsible for me actually being here today should be the one to confirm the news we had all been praying for. I explained to Joe and the realisation finally began to dawn. We were UP! And we were the CHAMPIONS! The mood around the ground suddenly became electric, with people hugging and cheering, and singing all manner of songs. It was the start of the promotion party that should have happened a week ago at Watford, cruelly taken away from us by the toxic air of uncertainty. Now that was all but forgotten, as the match against Leeds began to take on a whole new perspective. Win, lose or draw, we were back in the big time, we had effectively led from start to finish, and today was our day, or as Ian Holloway once said "Every dog has his day, and today is woof day!!!!".

We met Queenie outside the box office, as usual, and chatted about the incredible news. He played it all down, again, as usual, seemingly more interested in his programme than the small fact that we had just been promoted without even kicking a ball! The party really was in full swing, with chants of "Rangers are back, Rangers are back", and as we walked round the ground to take up our seats in the Ellerslie

Road stand, it finally sank in that this was the real deal. Inside the atmosphere was incredible, and when we finally reached our seats, each and every one had a flag on it. This was going to be one hell of a colourful day! As kick-off approached, the ground was awash with a sea of blue and white flags, and when the players entered, the roar was deafening! I would have been more than happy for the final whistle to go there and then and for them to bring on the trophy! But, before the directors were even out of the bar, Rangers took the lead, after just twenty-six seconds, with Tommy Smith striking a shot that Leeds keeper Kasper Schmeichel could only parry to Heider Helguson! 1-0!!!! It wasn't as if the crowd needed much lifting on a day like this, but we went absolutely mad anyway!

Alas, every silver lining has a cloud, and Leeds equalised after a defensive mix up on thirty-eight minutes, to send us in level at the break. The second half also proved to be an anti-climax, with Leeds grabbing the winner on sixty-eight minutes with a deflected shot. Regardless, our day wasn't about to be ruined by defeat – only our sixth in a fantastic season – and on the final whistle, the crowd erupted just as they would if we had won the match. The players shook hands and made a rapid exit as some fans (clearly unable to contain themselves, in spite of the threat of legal proceedings for entering the field of play and probably as a result of one or two too many *Heinekens* at half time) ran on to try and get to touch their heroes. The tannoy announcer tried in vain to get the over-excited supporters from the field, and in the end the stewards had to come in and clear the pitch. Only then was the *NPower Championship* podium brought in, bit by bit, and built around the centre of the pitch, the anticipation levels rising with it. Once in place, the announcement came that the players were returning, and as each was called out, a huge cheer greeted them. With everyone in place on the podium, it was just left for the talisman, Adel Taarabt, to saunter onto the scene.

The finale to the season was building to a crescendo and now was the moment we had all been waiting for. Home games, away days, agonised searches for streams. The text messages, battles with *QPR Player*, not to mention running the gauntlet in enemy territory. Over thirty years of waiting and never giving up hope climaxed into one perfect moment, as the trophy was handed to Adel to raise aloft against a backdrop of fireworks and fountains of Champagne to accompany the winners of the *NPower Championship* 2010-2011 – QUEENS PARK RANGERS!!!!

Joe and I hugged and it was truly a special feeling. How I would have loved to have called Mum and Dad at that moment. I know Mum would have been listening, back home in the kitchen on the blue elephant radio, sat perched on her chair, passing commentary back to Dad sitting in the lounge. Joe and I bounced up and down, waving our flags, and joining in with a few choruses of the customary song synonymous with winners, "We are the Champions" by Queen. Two years previously we had stood and watched as West Bromwich Albion had done the exact same thing on this very ground; last year it had been Newcastle. Now it was our turn. And all those moments of despair were forgotten.

As the players paraded the trophy round the pitch, milking the applause, I savoured it for all it was worth. Things like this don't happen very often to a club like Rangers, so when they do come along, you have to be there to make sure it all sinks in. As the players left the field, there was a further pitch invasion, and thousands gathered by the tunnel, desperate for another glimpse of the trophy and the heroes who had earned it. Joe wanted to go too and reluctantly I let him. Before I knew it, I was down there myself! I was about to take a photo when a fellow Hoop said "Go on mate, I'll take a photo of the two of you". It was one of those holiday abroad moments, when you suddenly trust a guy you have never met with three hundred notes of Panasonic TZ50 in his hot and sweaties, and the shot of me and Joe is truly legendary.

Once we were back in the largely deserted stand, Joe collected up as many discarded flags as he could lay his hands on, only pausing for Neil Warnock to take his turn and say a few words – an emotional final summing-up greeted with much cheering. And then it was time to go and meet Queenie outside the box office. It was a great moment for us both, with some sixty-six years' support amassed between us – over seventy with Joe in tow. As we made our way from the ground, Joe and I bought another flag, depicting our crest and declaring "We are Premier League". We waved it all the way to the station and on the train home, much to some other passengers' chagrin. On arrival at Norwich, we were met by a few Canaries still enjoying their promotion party. A bit of banter ensued, with yours truly simply waving the flags at them – all good-natured, for we both had something to cheer.

Me and Joe on the pitch

Watching the trophy being raised aloft that day was as much for my mum and dad as it was for me, Joe, Katie or Queenie, or for the many thousands of fans inside the stadium, or at home sat with their ears glued to *Player*, or listening intently to their radios (blue, elephant shaped or otherwise), or wherever they were, exiled around the globe. It was for all the hard miles on the road that every loyal Hoop does up and down the country, week in, week out. It was for every man, woman or child who calls themselves a fan of their team.

Joe, after promotion

In summary, M'Lord...

Supporting QPR is like being in a near perfect relationship. We have our ups and downs (the winning and the losing), the times when we are just ticking along (between matches), the falling out (inept performances and the feeling that those involved are not 'playing for the shirt'), and the making up (playing well and hopefully winning again). But you are always there for me. There's never any arguing back or cross words (although on occasion I may cuss and swear at you), and at times we have reached incredible highs. You never age and always strive to move with the changing times. I can honestly say that I love you unconditionally, yet you will never love me back in the same way. I forgive you all too easily, even when you let me down, because you make me feel like no other person, alive or deceased, can make me feel. I lavish money on you, yet you never pay your way, at least not financially. But I never want or need to look around for anyone else to take your place. Yes, I do look at others, I admit that. I am only human, and I do often admire from afar, sometimes even wishing you were perhaps a little more like them, but I would never want to change you, not even after thirty-odd years of being together. They say there are no guarantees in life, except for birth, death and taxes. Oh, and you building me up one week, only to let me down the next.

Supporting any team means they are with you for life. Players will come and go, some failing to endear themselves sufficiently to make it to the 'Legends Hall Of Fame', but our love for our club is unconditional. Just with our own lives, our club will see highs and lows, and just with our own lives, we have to tough out the hard times, often drawing on the team spirit of family and friends, while enjoying the good times, in the company of those we love the most.

And while my own inadequacies have plagued me for years, the sense that I always have to do more and be better than I was last time around, the one constant that has always been there, that's shaped my moods, picked me up when I most needed it, brought me down when I least required it, but whom I wouldn't change for any money, is Queens Park Rangers. For better, for worse, for richer, for poorer, in sickness and in health, until death do us part.

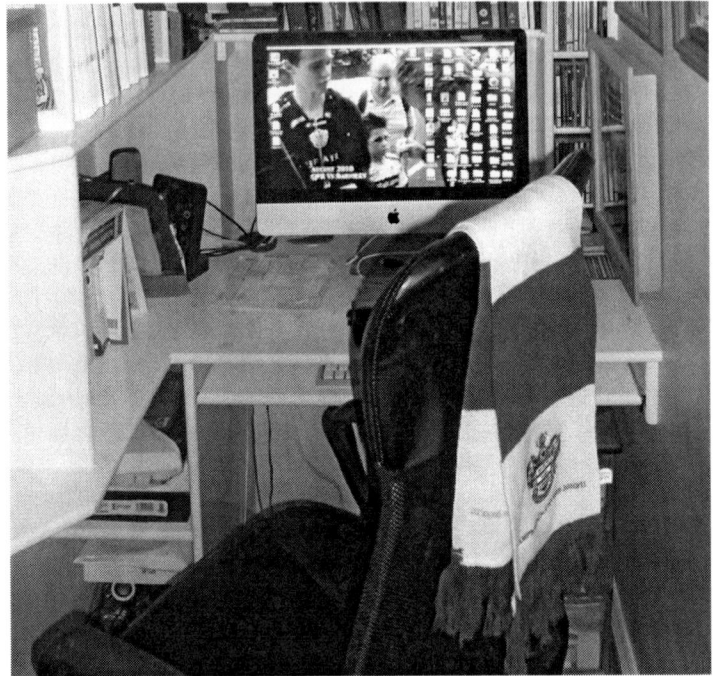

The infamous wheelie chair

90.00 The referee blows his whistle to end the Second Half

Epilogue...
Football's not a matter of life or death...

"God rest sleepy Jean, but no homecoming Queen"

QPR v Bolton Saturday August 13th, 2011: Our Premier League return...

Well, I have left these words for a further 24 hours from when I first intended to write, partly to allow emotions to die down a little, partly due to tiredness and partly because I just couldn't be arsed.

Yesterday was a day with a gamut of emotions for me. It should have been the great 'homecoming' back into the Premiership for my beloved Queens Park Rangers for the first time in sixteen years. History will show that it was anything but a welcome return, with the R's going down 4-0 at home to Bolton. And if yesterday had just been about the result then I should be sufficiently traumatised to be keeping the Samaritans open on my calls alone.

But if anything my reflections are about things other than the football.

The bulk of the Hartman clan, minus the current Mrs. H, left Norwich by train at 11.30am to begin our trip to the 'Smoke', both Joe and Katie resplendent in their replica kits from last season – Championship Champions 2010-2011 – seemingly a lifetime away now. Even if I had a spare £100 I couldn't replace them with the new season's shirts, as these have yet to be made. No sponsors announced as yet either, you see. We are a Premier League club with billionaire owners (who clearly accrue wealth by not spending), who have no connection with 'real' people – those of us who are 'working lower middle class', who enjoy watching a game of football and cheering on our heroes, donning our replica shirts with pride. Pie and a pint. Simple folk.

On arrival at Liverpool Street, we headed for the underground and what was to be Katie's first trip 'down under'. As we made our way to West London, some 14 stops or so, I asked her what she thought.

"Hot," was her short but rather accurate reply.

We disembarked in White City, surrounded by all shapes, sizes and designs of replica Rangers shirts from across the ages, and made our way through the estate. The kids played briefly in a small play park, letting off some steam and working off the effects of nearly a whole bag of *Starburst*. Then it was down the South Africa Road, past The Springbok public house, before us the familiar sight of the Loftus Road Stadium, with many hundreds of supporters mingling in the street, the familiar buzz of opening day expectation in the air, not to mention the smell of burgers. It was then that the day started to take on a difference for me.

You see, at this point, texts would normally be sent, calls would be made to determine whereabouts, and a meeting place finalised, commonly known as the 'apple'. With HRH. Queenie. Paul. My pal of 20 years. I can barely remember a game I didn't see him at. Certainly over that time he had always been there, and we had met up before, during or afterwards, to chat over new signings, formations, things that cheesed us off about our great club, the Board (no coincidence that I mentioned 'cheesed off' and 'the Board' in the same breath), anything and everything QPR. Only today I had no reason to make that call, as I knew he wouldn't answer. Oh, I still looked over at the box office, where we invariably used to meet, just to make sure he wasn't there. We still made our way along the outside of the stadium, down to the club shop and checked that he wasn't waiting there instead.

We popped in, to see last year's stock and the club's poor attempts at cashing in on the previous season's achievements, before exiting stage right and back out into the street, stopping again to purchase the match day programme. I half looked round to see if Paul wanted me to get his as well, but he didn't.

Continuing on, we made our way to the other side of the ground, to Ellerslie Road, and after the usual bag search and "You can't come in here with a half drunk bottle of *Morrison's* Isotonic" we entered the Mecca, filing slowly through the crowds, a waft of on tap-beer and betting puncturing the smoky air.

Once in our seats it was just like I always remember it, the familiar smell of a well groomed pitch, the tannoy announcements, the players warming up, Spark the mascot wandering around and waving at kids and adults alike. I looked across at the Upper Loft, just to check HRH had made it to his seat. But alas he hadn't.

Rather poignantly a wreath was laid in the centre circle before kick-off, for Jean Newman, a long-standing member of staff who passed away. How apt, for it could have been for so many others who had given their life to supporting their team over so many years.

The familiar sound of *London's Calling* by the Clash resonated around Loftus Road and then the announcer proclaimed "Less than 10 minutes to QPR's return to the Big Time!!!!". The giant screen illuminated with all those amazing images down the years, from the seventies sideburns era of Gerry and Stan, through the nineties and Clever Trevor and Sir Les, to last season's proudest moment in nearly thirty years and Adel lifting the trophy. With the cleverly chosen backing track and visual onslaught, it really makes the hairs on the back of your neck stick up, especially when you look at your own two children there, the next generation of Hoops. But what will Rangers look like as they are growing up?

Boutique football, I have heard bandied around, and already I am being priced out: £71 for the three of us for a category B match in only the third most expensive seats means that this will be pretty much a one-off and any other matches this season very carefully chosen. Then there's the travel at £37 and that's heavily discounted. It really isn't viable to watch a live match anymore. Not for the 'common people'.

Oh, there was a match as well. Contrary to what the final scoreline would suggest, we played well up until Bolton scored a one in one hundred strike, just before half time. In the second half we fell apart after 0-2 and ended up on the wrong end of a 0-4 mauling. But today it did feel different. As we made our way out of the ground and round to the other side, there was no after-match analysis to be had, no hanging back to collect a few new autographs, no lift to the station.

Instead, we headed back down South Africa Road and to the play park for the kids to have a few minutes' stretch before the journey home. Then the tube again before arriving at Liverpool Street and stopping off for the kids' favourite part of the day – Maccy D. Meals and drinks purchased, we made our way to our train and settled down to a slap-up tea, before the main leg, interspersed with games of *Uno*, *Rats on a Run, a Skateboard and a Scooter* on the *iPod* and a few games of *Mario* on the *DSi*.

Once back and on terra firma we headed for the car and home sweet home. Time to reflect, thumb the new look programme and try to put things into perspective. Katie made me a note, as she often does, which read:

> Dear daddy, I do like QPR but they lost for (four)
> nil. Love Katie.

Joe watched television.

And so, to some point to all of this, if you haven't already worked that one out yet. Yes, the match report will show who scored what, who played well, who didn't. But it will never reflect what goes on behind the scenes, the stories and the lives of those who make up the crowd.

I got to spend a day with my kids, at a place where I have so many memories, and that is a wonderful thing: being with people I love more than anything in a place I care about as much as anywhere. Yet today did feel different and I'm sad, almost resigned to say, that something has died within me too. I missed HRH today, I won't lie. His passing is something I guess I still haven't fully come to terms with. Not being able to share the result with him has left a void, and one I am not sure will ever be filled now. Sure, I will still follow the boys on, but maybe this is my time to step back a little and become that fan who watches from afar. I want my kids to grow up and take the tradition on, but only if that's what they want.

The great Bill Shankly was quoted as saying "Football's not a matter of life and death... it's more important than that". I hate to contradict one so knowledgeable of our great sport, but it isn't.

I touched on friendship at the start of this book, although HRH was much more than a friend in so many ways. He epitomised all the good times I can recall at Rangers over the years; many of the fondest memories involve him in some way. He was the *BBC World Service* when I couldn't get to matches, he was my 'go to' man for anything I needed to know about the club, my programme buyer, my signature collector, my expert summariser, my cab driver to and from the station before and after matches. I will miss his opening salutation of "How can I delight you?", when I called him for his after-match synopsis, interjected by a sudden outpouring of effing and blinding and questioning of the parentage of someone who had suddenly changed lanes and had the audacity to cut him up.

But above all, I miss you because you were my friend. I hope your seat in Heaven Block next to my mum and dad affords you the view of Premiership football you deserve, and I am so pleased you saw the R's go up in style for what proved to be your last hurrah. But hey, what a way to go! You may be gone in body, but your undying spirit and love for the R's will never be forgotten. Somehow I just know that my following of the R's will never truly be the same again.

May you rest in peace HRH.

For we have to cherish those we have and remember those who sadly can't make the trip with us any more.

Friendship. Family. And Football.

Joe and Katie v Bolton

The referee blows his whistle to end extra time

Doing it for the kids
Chris Charles

It's the dream of every football-loving dad to one day see his child play for the team he loves. For me it's a case of when, not if.

It's not that little Lois is being touted as the next Wayne Rooney (even Arsenal don't take on under-2s – yet) but having Down's syndrome, she qualifies to play for the QPR Tiger Cubs – a side made up entirely of children born with the condition.

Lois

Of course, Lois has to learn to walk first (at 23 months she has perfected the fine art of bum-shuffling) but when she reaches the magical age of seven, she'll be turning up at Tiger Cubs HQ decked out in the blue and white hoops – whether she wants to or not.

QPR are one of six football clubs in England who run teams for children with Down's syndrome - Fulham, Charlton, Manchester United, Hereford and West Ham make up the rest – and supporters of the scheme are confident these numbers will continue to grow.

Patricia James, corporate fundraising officer for the Down's Syndrome Association, said: "It all started when a colleague of mine spoke to Fulham in 2006 about disability football. A pilot scheme for the Fulham Badgers was launched later that year, and it got a fantastic response.

"We had been getting feedback from parents of children with Down's syndrome who couldn't find any sporting activity for them to do. Eighty five per cent of these children are enrolled in mainstream primary schools, but when it comes to physical activity they often get left on the sidelines because their oxygen intake is up to 40% less.

"With this initiative, the children are becoming more active

209

and gaining confidence. It's also very important for their emotional and social development. Unlike sport in the mainstream schools, it's a level playing field for everyone and they can take what they learn on the training pitches into the classroom and everyday life."

QPR Community Trust chief executive Andy Evans, who oversees the Tiger Cubs, concurs. "It's been phenomenal," he said. "The kids get an incredible amount of satisfaction, a sense of belonging, and it provides a support network for the parents where they can share common experiences.

"I've heard stories of children in mainstream education being called up in assembly wearing their QPR kit and the whole school giving them a round of applause because they're playing for the Tiger Cubs."

Training sessions are held every Monday night and the most difficult task facing the coaches is getting the children to leave the pitch at the end.

Head coach Adam Finch explained: "We try to keep the sessions as energetic as we can and we also have a fundamental group where we concentrate more on the motor skills – running, skipping, jumping, that sort of stuff.

"It's fantastic, always good fun. Some football sessions can get a bit stale, but never with the Tiger Cubs. It's always new, fresh and exciting – and if the kids are excited, you can't help but get excited as well."

The scheme first came to my attention last year, when the team showed off their skills during a half-time display at Loftus Road. The crowd were right behind them, cheering every goal that went in, and the kids milked the applause that came their way.

I'd be lying if I said it didn't bring a tear to my eye, but it also made me realise that any preconceptions I had about Lois not being able to do the things other children took for granted were misplaced. Let's face it, after coming through major heart surgery at three months old and having to be fed through a tube for a year, kicking a football around should be a doddle.

We didn't know Lois was going to be born with Down's syndrome – in fact after the 12-week scan, the nurse confidently predicted there was a one in 8,000 chance – so when we found out it was a shock to say the least. But you learn to adapt and nearly two years on, I can honestly say I wouldn't have her any other way.

Birmingham City midfielder Lee Carsley, whose 11-year-old son, Connor, has Down's syndrome, agrees. "You can get burdened down with it or take it in your stride," he said. "Of course you still think about it every day but if you lay in bed worrying about it all night you'd never be able to get anything done.

"I treat all my kids the same – I'm no different to any other Dad. I love them all – although sometimes they can be a pain!"

Carsley is a tireless fundraiser in his role as patron of the Solihull Down's syndrome support group and is in talks with Birmingham's new owners about the possibility of setting up a team in the mould of the Tiger Cubs.

He said: "I think it's a really good thing for the kids and can only be beneficial. Connor goes on some football coaching classes but they're all at different levels and he sometimes gets left behind.

"He's proud of me and what I do but while my other kids understand my role, Connor's a bit of a glory hunter. He wants me to score a goal and that's it. It would break his heart if he knew I haven't scored many!"

Carsley's former Everton team-mate Kevin Kilbane is patron of the DSActive charity, encouraging children with Down's syndrome to get involved in sport, and is heavily involved in promoting teams like the Fulham Badgers and QPR Tiger Cubs.

The Hull midfielder, who won his 103rd cap for the Republic of Ireland against Brazil, has a five-year-old daughter, Elsie, with Down's syndrome, and handed out the medals when the Badgers and Cubs recently teamed up to play a visiting Hong Kong XI.

"It's a really important scheme and it's gaining momentum by the week," he said. "The work the team has put in has been phenomenal, but it would be great to get more kids involved. At the moment there's not that much competition for the children with Down's syndrome or any other disability and I'd love every club to one day have its own team."

As for Lois, she turns two on 9 April, meaning it will be a mere 1,825 days before I finally get the chance to see her in action for the Tiger Cubs. The first two years of her life have coincided with extraordinary goings-on at my club that have seen a succession of managers come and go, leaving a team tipped for promotion embroiled in a relegation battle.

The changing of the guard in the boardroom, coupled with the arrival of football's Mr Motivator, Neil Warnock, will hopefully steady the ship, although even Warnock would struggle to replicate the drive and enthusiasm shown by the Cubs.

Indeed some of the footballing prima donnas ticked off by England coach Fabio Capello last week could do worse than pop down to witness this unbridled passion first-hand. And not a WAG or a Ferrari in sight.

Originally posted on http://www.bbc.co.uk/blogs/chrischarles/2010/03/doing_it_for _the_kids.html; Monday, 8 March 2010.

About the author...

Frederick RJ Hartman (or Fred to his friends) was born in Kingsbury, Middlesex on August 27th, 1968 (just in case you wanted to send him a card). He is married to Kerri (the current Mrs. Hartman), and has two children, Joseph (the J in RJ, not coincidentally), who is ten, and seemingly getting older every year, and Katie, who is seven, and seemingly close to leaving home.

It has always been his wish to write a book worthy of publication, ever since writing *The Diary of a Witch's Cat* when around nine years old. While it did get laminated, it never got published, and the only ever copy is still knocking around in his loft somewhere.

Fred also writes regularly for his website www.writesaidfred.co.uk (see what he did there?) and can normally be found at home writing something or other, his talents ranging from blogs to song lyrics, poems and rather more detailed than necessary shopping lists. More recently, he has co-written the much acclaimed sitcom *It's a Bankers Life for Me* with long-term writing partner Clive, as well as two excellent radio shows entitled *People Watching*. He says "I'd love to tell you how successful these have been, but sadly nobody has come back to us yet, so I can't!"

Fred would one day like to write full time. As in get paid for it. Although some breaks would also be welcome.

"Some men are born great. Some achieve greatness and some have greatness thrust upon them."

Then of course there is Fred Hartman.

With thanks...

I would like to thank a few people in particular for their special help in making the book what you see before you today.

Nigel and Debs at Beaten Track Publishing, for their tireless work in editing (OK Debs, rewriting, but we won't tell everyone our secret!), marketing, technical competence and Sunday morning Skype breakfast meetings. I can honestly say I could not have done it without you both and actually mean that sincerely. Oh, and thanks Beth for a young person's perspective on things as well as being a next generation Hoop!

Kaitlyn Neve, for her unbelievable photography skills and the ability to take my ideas and make them worth looking at! Thanks for your patience and having to listen to me on the phone while I drone on about concepts, colours, fading and effects when clearly I have no idea what the hell I am talking about!

Rod Marsh, for not only writing a foreword for the book, but for being in the elite group of players able to call themselves true Rangers legends.

Jim Luck, for being a most humble and generous friend to both me and Joe over the years, and for being Rangers through and through.

The Tiger Cubs, for showing us all how to simply enjoy the game for what it is. Perhaps we should all take a few moments out to remember that next time we are screaming at someone to play better.

NaNoWriMo (aka the National Novel Writing Month), for helping focus me in the month of November so I could get down over 45k words in the space of about twenty days. Had I not achieved this, it may well have been another forty-three years before the book actually came out.

ightning Source UK Ltd.
iilton Keynes UK
KOW050350050712

95513UK00001B/11/P

To Clive Grooms, friend and comedy writing partner, for actually focusing me on what subject to write about initially. Eight days in to November, and with a blank page still sitting in front of me, he said "If I was going to write a book in thirty days I would write about something I know and am passionate about". After explaining that I didn't believe I could write fifty thousand words on sex chat lines and Indonesian matchmaking sites he simply said "QPR". And the rest is contained in the book you are holding.

And lastly, and by no means least, to all those people (football loving or otherwise) who have come into my life at one time or another and who I can honestly call friends, including but not exclusively, those who have put me up / put up with me crashing on their sofas (leather or otherwise) before / after various matches down the years. As my mum always used to say "It is better to be able to count your true friends on the fingers of one hand than to have many that call themselves friends and not be there for you".

This book is truly for anyone who has ever loved, lost or won.

Extra Content...

Instructions:

Scan the QR Code below with your mobile phone (you may need to install a barcode scanner app first) free extra content - our way of thanking you for p this book.

With thanks...

I would like to thank a few people in particular for their special help in making the book what you see before you today.

Nigel and Debs at Beaten Track Publishing, for their tireless work in editing (OK Debs, rewriting, but we won't tell everyone our secret!), marketing, technical competence and Sunday morning Skype breakfast meetings. I can honestly say I could not have done it without you both and actually mean that sincerely. Oh, and thanks Beth for a young person's perspective on things as well as being a next generation Hoop!

Kaitlyn Neve, for her unbelievable photography skills and the ability to take my ideas and make them worth looking at! Thanks for your patience and having to listen to me on the phone while I drone on about concepts, colours, fading and effects when clearly I have no idea what the hell I am talking about!

Rod Marsh, for not only writing a foreword for the book, but for being in the elite group of players able to call themselves true Rangers legends.

Jim Luck, for being a most humble and generous friend to both me and Joe over the years, and for being Rangers through and through.

The Tiger Cubs, for showing us all how to simply enjoy the game for what it is. Perhaps we should all take a few moments out to remember that next time we are screaming at someone to play better.

NaNoWriMo (aka the National Novel Writing Month), for helping focus me in the month of November so I could get down over 45k words in the space of about twenty days. Had I not achieved this, it may well have been another forty-three years before the book actually came out.

To Clive Grooms, friend and comedy writing partner, for actually focusing me on what subject to write about initially. Eight days in to November, and with a blank page still sitting in front of me, he said "If I was going to write a book in thirty days I would write about something I know and am passionate about". After explaining that I didn't believe I could write fifty thousand words on sex chat lines and Indonesian matchmaking sites he simply said "QPR". And the rest is contained in the book you are holding.

And lastly, and by no means least, to all those people (football loving or otherwise) who have come into my life at one time or another and who I can honestly call friends, including but not exclusively, those who have put me up / put up with me crashing on their sofas (leather or otherwise) before / after various matches down the years. As my mum always used to say "It is better to be able to count your true friends on the fingers of one hand than to have many that call themselves friends and not be there for you".

This book is truly for anyone who has ever loved, lost or won.

Extra Content...

Instructions:

Scan the QR Code below with your mobile phone / device (you may need to install a barcode scanner app first) to access free extra content - our way of thanking you for purchasing this book.

Lightning Source UK Ltd.
Milton Keynes UK
UKOW050350050712

195513UK00001B/11/P